The Practicing Church
by
Donald Llewellyn Roberts

Christian Publications, Inc.
Harrisburg, Pennsylvania

Christian Publications, Inc.
25 S. 10th Street, P.O. Box 3404
Harrisburg, PA 17105

© 1981 by Christian Publications, Inc. All rights reserved
Library of Congress Catalog Card Number: 01-67318
ISBN: 0-87509-303-5
Scripture quotations from the *New American Standard Bible*, © The Lockman Foundation, 1960, 1962, 1963, 1968, 1971, 1972, 1973, 1975, are used by permission.
Quotations from THE NEW INTERNATIONAL VERSION, NEW TESTAMENT © 1973 by The New York Bible Society International are used by permission.
Printed in the United States of America

Contents

Prologue

1

Pilgrim and the Big Meeting

Behold, A Pilgrim and his wife went forth to a church meeting.

"Are we ever glad to see you two tonight. You bring us to the quorum for the meeting. Besides, it's nice to have new members interested in the church." All of this gushed out of the Minister of Business Administration as his look of concern melted into one of relaxation. "And to think you didn't even come to the steak fry. Steak fries have always done it at this church. The only time we missed reaching a quorum was the night the teen-agers prepared the supper and served pizzas with limburger cheese."

Pilgrim, as a relatively new pilgrim, thought all of this to be strange conversation coming just before the church's Big Meeting of the year. That meeting, now made official by their presence, was called to order by the moderator, who also happened to be the pastor. Dr. R. Roland Ruhles was the epitome of church authority. He also was the resident mogul on conducting well-ordered church business meetings. An unconfirmed rumor had it that the grandfather of Dr. Ruhles, Remaliah Ruhles, had actually attended school with the renowned Robert, and had added many valued insights to Robert's book of parliamentary procedure.

There was yet one hitch to getting underway. Dr. Ruhles invariably asked retired millionaire Deacon Duncan to open the meeting with prayer. Deacon Duncan had that distinctive ability to gather up all the tidbits of current church news and then blend them with extensive references to Old Testament passages, a mixture which always gave his prayers a folksy, apocalyptic flavor.

Some of the less spiritual members of the church claimed that they averaged half a pack of Life Savers during the course of such supplications. All agreed that the year 1976 had seen the high water mark of Deacon Duncan's career. It had been marked by a Bicentennial-sized prayer which seemed to last for two hundred years and which left little uncovered. Needless to say, on this the night of the Big Meeting, Deacon Duncan did not fall short of anyone's expectations.

Pilgrim had determined beforehand that attending the Big Meeting was vital if he were to catch the pulse of the church. It did seem to him that the minutes took an hour to read and accept. This was a side of church life he had not sampled here. It reminded him of a board meeting at his company.

"Now we shall proceed to a consideration of the church budgets," intoned Dr. Ruhles. He spoke with that confident ease of a man who had been this route many times and who knew exactly how the script would unfold. Pilgrim gasped as he saw that the church budget was $2,356,812.14. Much of this was allocated for the fifty-eight staff members, seven of whose names were Ruhles.

"Are there any questions on the budget?" Dr. Ruhles spoke as if his question were rhetorical. "Yes," called out a brave soul from the side. "Why does Pastor Shear need two new cars this year, a Lincoln Continental and a Datsun?"

Quickly the resident Director of Church Explosion interposed, almost apologetic that someone would question a budget item which had come by direct pulmonary inspiration from the Board of Rulers, which board was chaired by Dr. Ruhles. "You see, our Minister of Sheep Securing must be all things to all men in order to gain some. Therefore, he must be able to relate to up-and-outers as well as down-and-outers; hence these vehicles will enable him to cruise with comfortable identification in any part of our fair community."

"Any further questions?" None forthcoming, Dr. Ruhles moved the adoption of the budget, which was accomplished without dissent. Next came the missionary budget. By comparison this was a paltry $1,500,000. Pilgrim was intrigued by the variety of this church's missionary involvement. Included was a sum of $25,000 for Dr. Ruhles's upcoming Arctic adventure, an evangelistic trek amongst nomadic Eskimos. The year before had seen his Waikiki Witness mission to the surf set. The church had even underwritten passage for the popular TV Gospel group, the Singing Surfbards, who accompanied the Doctor.

Surely, thought Pilgrim, here was a man who spared no cost in accomplishing his ministry.

"What very specialized interests they have here," commented Mrs. Pilgrim to her husband. Special indeed, for there on the list were support amounts for the Mission to Displaced Left-handed Lithuanians as well as for Dogmatic Dogfights, Inc. The latter was an outreach to former World War II fighter pilots. Yes, there seemed to be something for everyone.

As the Big Meeting progressed, the Pilgrims were surprised to see how well orchestrated everything was. Their little old church back home had often been the scene of some knock down, drag out church spats where the faithful would become embroiled in controversy, usually over peripheral matters. However, the brethren managed to agree to disagree, to love each other despite differences, and to achieve a balance of power which kept interest alive and congregational polity active.

The two major budgets passed, old and new business matters were then entertained. Unanimously, the congregation voted a six-month sabbatical for the Doctor to write his memoirs *Ruhles in the Game of Life* and also to tour the sun-belt conference circuit showing his epic slide presentation *Bringing Light to Liechtenstein*. This eighty-nine minute classic had already won two religious media awards and had kept the Doctor away from the church for weeks at a time. In deference to economy it was decided that the staff would again fill in for Dr. Ruhles in his absence.

Pilgrim reflected on these goings-on. This wasn't quite what he had expected. Seated in the well-appointed fellowship hall, recently named Ruhles's Ramparts, it seemed to Pilgrim that there should be more deliberation over such large appropriations of money, and that the apparently unmentionable subject of the Doctor's prolonged absences should also be open to scrutiny. He wondered about one man's having so much authority in what he understood to be an institution started by the Lord. Why had these members, robot-like, passively allowed so much to go unchallenged? It just didn't ring true. Something, or was it Someone, was missing!

His musings were suddenly interrupted by the soft voice of a young woman. "Dr. Ruhles, we need some new equipment in the primary department." The Doctor blanched as the staff members turned white with dismay. Someone was challenging the Doctor's budget, even after it had been adopted!

Order was restored quickly as motions were motioned, seconds seconded, amendments amended, and chunks of verbiage laid on the table, and then slid off the table to committees for further study. For a brief instant the personal element had almost sidetracked the ecclesiastical juggernaut, but with sanity back in control, parliamentary palaver spared the church an ugly admission—the possibility that the good Doctor and his Board of Rulers had overlooked something for the welfare of the flock.

"I guess I should be more excited about these budgets and this program," Pilgrim said to Mrs. Pilgrim after the Big Meeting had been smartly and snappily adjourned. "But isn't a church composed of the called-out ones, and shouldn't they also have the right to be 'calling out ones' in the church's business? Maybe some of those hassles we had back home over carpeting the sanctuary or paving the parking lot were more electrifying than edifying, but at least the people were a part of the decision-making process."

"Well," observed Mrs. Pilgrim, "maybe that's the way it's done here. Maybe the people are so busy with their lives that they let the Doctor and his board make the decisions for them. After all, he is the professional. And it certainly is a lot quicker. Why, tonight they touched all the congregational bases and voted on almost four million dollars in less than three hours. Our old church would have needed the entire Millennium to vote on that much money!"

Just then the Minister of Business Administration passed by, looking not unlike the proverbial cat. "Forgive the terminology," he said, "but I'll bet you've never been in a smoother business meeting than this one. Of course we had that unfortunate power grab attempt near the end, but we fought that off. That's where Dr. Ruhles's knowledge of Robert's comes in handy. Do you know that many of us see a prophetic cast to the Doctor's name? To us, R. Roland Ruhles stands for 'Our

11

Roland Rules.' How we have prospered under his leadership!"

It was a pensive Pilgrim who maneuvered down the freeway. The Big Meeting, as last week's bulletin had called it, was now a matter of history. But he sensed a gnawing uneasiness. In terms of growth, size, momentum, and the present age, this certainly must be the way to run a booming church—or is it? Yet for all the appearance of progress, something—or is it Someone—is missing.

But who was he to question the power structure of this church, and how could he possibly argue with such success?

2

The Practicing Church

"Our Roland rules." Such, too often, is the case in local churches. Be it by congregational default or clerical dynamism, many churches focus on a man-centered rule. The preceding chapter has obviously overstated the case. Even in the most dynastic of church situations, there remains breathing room for service by laymen. But the fictitious church business meeting just described is not that far removed from reality. There is an increased striving toward the goal of becoming a booming church. Many of the same are controlled by dominant pastoral figures who delegate or relegate their duties to staffs of professionals.

For those who still hold to more congregational participation, there is something unsettling to observe a person with a program usurp and stifle the spontaneity of congregational involvement. Are laymen so busy that they must turn over the actual control of a church to religious professionals? Are not large staffs an unacknowledged admission of weakness? How do we square this with the current interest in the gifts of the Spirit? Where and how will gifted laymen serve if churches become top-heavy with professionals?

The human side of church life is better described as amateur than professional. This is not to opt for the amateurish whereby the work of the Lord is done in a careless fashion. Instead, it means a recognition that in the handling of holy matters, we are continually learning, always growing though not "arriving." Even in the endlessness of eternity we shall continue to be servants and students, ever plumbing the divine depths.

Thus the expression "The Practicing Church" is rooted in the realization that the Church is to pursue God-given priorities, practicing what it believes yet aware of its own learning experience. Its reliance must be on a source of authority beyond itself, though revealed through itself.

In the sports realm the dictum is practice. Athletic teams constantly practice. No matter how efficient their last performance may have been, they return to the gyms or the fields for more preparation. Though teams attain varying degrees of proficiency, their coaches are never satisfied. They desire to hone skills to a finer edge by eliminating errors of omission or commission. The same is true in the area of medicine. Doctors actually call their work a practice. Although they have achieved high levels of competency through years of rigorous study and internship, still they continue to sharpen their skills in their "practice."

A negative side to this concept, as related to the church, is the tendency for believers to haunt the practice field rather than the playing field. In such cases they inhabit church facilities and functions to spectate or study with little real application of the learned precepts to daily life. Someone has spoken of this as being "unexperienced truth."

But the idea of practicing envisioned in this book springs from its simplest of definitions—the application of knowledge. Herein lies a problem. Religious expertise may be achieved, yet it can leave a hollowness without that dimension which only the certifying and authoritative presence of God can give. High levels of even evangelical performance characterized by suave, sharp, modern Adams leave one wondering whether the Lord has not become superfluous in such situations.

Nothing radically new will leap from the pages of this book, rather a recasting of old and enduring truths. The beginning section, "Standing," considers the what of the church. What should the church be doing? It incorporates a wistful invitation to return to the starting point by obtaining new bearings from old principles. In order to stand, we must stop. Thus the section repeats elemental concerns. The whats of the church include simplicity of life, areas for service, principles related to people, and the primacy of the Word of God.

The second section, "Seeking," sets forth the distinctly God-centered stance the practicing church must take to avoid gradual drift toward a man-oriented pulpit and pew. A call is sounded to reaffirm cardinal truths about the preeminence of the Lord in His Church. Delicate, though demanding, issues are raised about the anguish, the anger, the awe, and the authority of God. These issues are vital, for only in the paradox of finding yet ever seeking can spiritual vitality and balance be maintained.

The third section, "Serving," returns to the application of divine knowledge. Independent, yet blending into a thematic continuity, these chapters antiphonally reveal key facets of ministry and mandate for the practicing church, as viewed in a corporate and individual sense.

The epilogue relates a recent natural phenomenon to the awesome power of God and stands as a reminder of both the grace and the grandeur of our God. In an increasingly anthropocentric culture and age, this event serves to warn the Church of the might and the majesty of "Him with Whom we have to do," even the One who is the head of the Church.

I.   Standing

3

The Simple Life

The simple life. Is it a dream? A mirage of the ages? Is the quest for the simple life a delusive ploy to escape reality? Should one retreat to the mountains, live from the land, and in returning to nature seek to evade the hollowness of much of modern life? By definition, the word *simple* suggests being "free from complexity, uncomplicated, innocent, unsophisticated." Is it simplistic to think that life can be made simple?

Paul explored the possibility of the simple life in the Book of Second Corinthians. As the apostle wrestled with internal and external dangers to the church at Corinth, he sought to call the people back to a life of simplicity. The word *simplicity* which he used had an interesting background. Carried over into the English, the word is *haplot*. The *haplot* was a Greek soldier, an infantryman. His training was rigorous and very basic; his mission, not complex. Essentially, that mission related to finding the enemy and destroying him.

The first century *haplot* was physically hardened, a human weapon skilled in hand-to-hand combat. He mastered a few concepts and strove for survival. He was always harking back to the basics. Thus when the apostle used this word, he was not urging softness or indecision, but rather a simplicity rooted in spiritual maturity and endurance.

R.E.O. White, in his *52 Seed Thoughts for Christian Living*, considered the implications of such a simplicity when he wrote, "We must not defend a willful laziness and emptiness of mind by miscalling it 'simplicity.' Yet when all is said an opposite danger remains. We moderns are tempted to delight in complexities; we emit a smokescreen of discussion and alternative definitions, of complicated arguments and many-sided questions, to hide us from the duty of making up our minds. Simplicity pleads to be heard. It often finds the way while the experts are still searching their maps."[1]

The Church needs to be called back to a biblical simplicity which is neither simplistic nor simple-minded. In admonishing the Corinthians, Paul called them to simplicity in three crucial areas.

He first urged upon them the importance of simplicity in their relationships. Basic to all of life is one's relationship to the Lord. In his salutation, Paul had invoked, "grace to you and peace from God our Father, and from the Lord Jesus Christ" (2 Cor. 1:2). Their faith in the finished work of Christ had resulted in grace and peace from God, the outward work of Christ producing the inward benefice in their lives. A result of their faith in Christ then was "simplicity and godly sincerity" as 2 Corinthians 1:12 declared. Paul had not come to them as a created product of a human media, but rather as a re-created personification of divine mercy. Some have desired to equate simplicity with the thought of holiness of life. There need be no disagreement, for both ideas are conveyed. Singlemindedness, a relaxing in the very being of God with a resulting transluscence of life, supplies the ingredients which are the backdrop to personal holiness.

The apostolic example was to be reflected in other relationships. Christians were to be frank and open in their dealings with the world. They were to be "wise as serpents, yet simple as doves" (Matt. 10:16) in dealing with the lost. They were to be involved yet detached, in but not of a world system which so often threatened to engulf them. And then, as Paul, they were to be spontaneously honest with the brethren—no, not in the way of current sensitivity fads. There are personal preserves in life not intended for public consumption. Still Christians need a controlled freedom in fellowship, and that comes only as they 'simply' relax in the Lord and produce a comparably relaxed companionship in the church.

Christians need this desperately. They are driven between the extremes of insensitivity and rote clichés in much which passes for sharing. But how can such a refreshingly simple life be achieved? Paul pointed to the answer in 2 Corinthians 1:9-10, where he wrote of an event in his life which nearly resulted in his death. That answer resided in the paradox that death produces life, a concept clearly enunciated in Galatians 2:20. Thus death to the self-life in all of its ensnaring forms enables the very life of Christ to radiate through these earthen vessels. Then the Christian, with no ego or image to defend, can really be himself in Christ, free from religious jargon and stilted piety. How sad that we who shall spend forever together find it so difficult to communicate now in the life of the church.

A second apostolic imperative involved the matter of simplicity in service. How insightful that Paul would choose one particular area as the test case for his thesis. He began with allusion to the grace of God bestowed on the churches in Macedonia and then launched into an extensive discussion of material stewardship. His concern was to jog the memories of the Corinthians to receive an offering for the poor in Jerusalem. He impaled their slow response on the horns of Judean need and the Macedonian example.

The key to it all is the thrust of 2 Corinthians 8:5, "They gave themselves first to the Lord" (NIV). Issuing out of that commitment was the contribution of their substance. Three times (2 Cor. 8:2; 9:11, 13) Paul used the Greek word *haplot*, each time with a slightly different meaning. *Haplot* basically means simple. He injected into the idea of simplicity the companion thought of generosity. Even though these Macedonians had endured civil war, Roman oppression, and persecution, they still had given from their little with a bounteous simplicity. And that is the pattern for all service, be it spiritual or substantive. Love for Christ, rooted in a relaxed posture with God, leads to an unrestrained generosity.

Their generosity sprang from the recognition of a more profound generosity, "For ye know the grace of our Lord Jesus Christ, that, though he was rich, yet for your sakes he became poor, that ye through his poverty might be rich" (2 Cor. 8:9). Thus the generosity of our service for Christ is reflective of the simplicity of our relationship to Christ.

How vital this is! We need deliverance from the pious legalism which enslaves us to religious schedules rather than allowing a ripening relationship with the Lord. When will we let the saints escape from the treadmill of services, seminars, and special speakers to cultivate the kind of inner life which will result in a more radiant outer life of service?

There was a third area which deeply concerned Paul as he urged simplicity upon the Corinthian fellowship. He longed to see simplicity in their doctrine. The closing chapters of this epistle have provoked much debate. Almost without pause, the apostle moved from pastoral concern to public confrontation. The issue was his apostolic authority. Needless to say, he was not concerned about carving out some private domain of influence in Corinth. He did not need letters of commendation, for the Corinthians composed his own letter, written not with pen but by the very finger of the living God.

Paul seemed gripped with a holy anger at the possibility of false teachers, leading the Corinthian believers astray. He was jealous and even "feared" that they would be seduced doctrinally from that "simplicity that is in Christ" (2 Cor. 11:3). Paul would be equally distressed today, for that false angel of light has covered many minds with a veneer of seeming truth. In so many cases deflection has arisen from slipping aside from that simplicity which is found in Christ.

Somehow we have become more taken with the gifts than the Giver, more absorbed in charismatic men than the charismatic Spirit (1 John 2:20). He points us to Christ, and that is where the simplicity of our doctrine must reside. Such doctrine focuses on the person of Christ. "For we preach not ourselves, but Christ Jesus the Lord; and ourselves your servants for Jesus' sake" (2 Cor. 4:5). How the church needs concentrated preaching on Jesus Christ! We are so busy hawking our methods and success stories that we hardly have time left for "the despised and rejected One." A haplot-like doctrine also provides a corrective perspective. It gets our eyes on the eternal (2 Cor. 4:18), for it shows us how tenuous our hold on life actually is (2 Cor. 5:1). Finally, such basic teaching reminds us of the dynamic resident within our lives. A spiritual explosion has made us totally new creations, and a radical new process of change has begun (2 Cor. 5:17).

The centuries have only magnified the importance of sound and simple doctrine. Beware of appearance, of sharp and smooth individuals whose expertise does not exalt Christ but rather inflates themselves and their ministries, not His. As Paul developed this thesis of simplicity, he moved from what we are to what we do, and then revealed the fountain of both—what we believe.

Our Lord was also exercised about this matter of simplicity, for He said, "The light of the body is the eye: if therefore thine eye be single, thy whole body shall be full of light" (Matt. 6:22). The word *single* is the same root word, *haplot*, often rendered *simple*. Singleness of purpose leads to simplicity of life!

We need to become twentieth century haplots —simple in our relationships via an honesty with the Lord, the brethren, and the world. We need to recapture a holy enthusiasm for glorifying and serving the Lord. We need a renewed emphasis on Christ-centered doctrine as we peel away the layers of marginal matters in our churches. There needs to be spiritual dieting to trim our lives and schedules so that the Spirit again can have access to our minds and our wills.

Paul did not call the Corinthians to vague visions and vapid dreams. He urged upon them a life style anchored in holy simplicity. Such a goal should also be a priority in our complex times. R.E.O. White well summarized this need: "We make every issue of faith and conduct a matter of enquiry until we lose the reality of the Christian life in all our talking about it."[2] The church will take a giant step in the direction of simplicity when it recognizes its mandate to produce saints, not conversation and statistics.

Indeed, let all of us be careful lest we, ever so subtly, be drawn away from that simplicity which is found only in Christ!

---

1. R.E.O. White, *52 Seed Thoughts for Christian Living* (Grand Rapids: Wm. B. Eerdmans Publishing Company, 1963), p. 104.
2. Ibid.

4

Tale of Three Worlds

For the Christian, life is the Tale of Three Worlds. In these worlds he spends the 168 hours which make up each week. If we deduct the hours for sleeping, we begin to get a picture of an individual's priorities as we see where he expends this precious currency called time. How do we spend our/His 168 hours?

Paul enabled us to gain an overview of these three worlds in his Epistle to the Colossians. He actually gave us a biblical philosophy of life. Moving from the external to the internal, we can observe biblical principles for the way we ought to live.

The first of these worlds is the outer world. A number of ingredients make up this particular sphere of involvement. One's vocation immediately comes to mind. Not only the Christian worker, but also the layman must realize that his job is a calling. Luther wrote, "Work is sacred." Both digging ditches and digging into the Word involve effort and time. The layman, who is also a priest unto God, certainly needs the assurance that God has placed him where he is. Each of us has a task to accomplish. We must not demean the man who earns his way in that outer world by suggesting that he is a second-class citizen in the kingdom.

Paul singled out servants in Colossians 3:22 and admonished them to be good workers, not trying to gain the favor of men, but rather the favor of God. The apostle could scarcely have reached lower in the social structure, for such servants attached to households were often at the mercy of their masters' whims. Then in verses 23-24, Paul indicated the responsibility and reward which issued from this servant/master relationship. The servant was to do his best as unto the Lord.

The everyday world has increasingly become a civilized jungle. Laymen are at the cutting edge as they contact people on a daily basis. Yet the "professional" clergy so often are out of touch with that world. Launched from insulated, if not isolated enclaves, clerical preaching and teaching smacks of an unreal world. Sabbaticals in an office or factory could well serve to bring many preachers back into touch with this outer world.

Education is another part of the outer world. To educate means "to lead out" from ignorance to understanding. Life is a learning process. Whether formally or informally, we are constantly learning. Jobs today demand more in terms of continuing education. However, significant as they are, degrees do not make the man. There is something about the furnace of practical experience which "book larnin" can never replace. The Christian wants to be skilled in his field of endeavor, yet always with the counterbalance of spiritual

27

education.

From that outer world of education must come the balance which enables the Christian to keep his bearings. Paul pointed the way in the beginning of his prayer in Colossians 1:9-10. He longed to see these believers "filled with the knowledge of his will" while they were "increasing in the knowledge of God." His frame of reference was Christ, "in Whom are hid all the treasures of wisdom and knowledge," (Col. 2:3). With such a center, learning has purpose, a constant relating of truth and truths to our growing knowledge of the living God.

An increasingly important area of life in the outer world is recreation. The word implies renewal. The paradox is that in modern parlance, recreation is often linked with vacation, which means to leave empty. The gospel story of the self-reformation of the demon-possessed who then was repossessed by a larger company of demons bears well on this recreation/vacation contradiction. Some companies have begun offering their employees four-day weekends as they compact working hours into fewer days in order to allow for more leisure. Such pleasure-oriented practices certainly have a relationship to increased mobility, unreliability, divorce, energy consumption, and lack of vocational commitment. And the extended weekend has also impacted upon the church as well.

The Christian really does not have this kind of "free" time. All of his time was purchased on the cross; thus Paul admonished, "And whatever you do in word or deed, do all in the name of the Lord Jesus, giving thanks through Him to God the Father," (Col. 3:17, NASB). For many believers, recreation/vacation turns into a wilderness experience, though it could become a vehicle for new contacts for Christ. Should we shun the word *vacation* and think more of purposeful relaxation? Vance Havner wrote, "Come apart for a while, or you'll come apart in a while." But this area of the outer world needs to be controlled and examined frequently, for it is a dangerous one. Remember Jonah's booking passage on a Mediterranean cruise, but doing so deliberately to avoid his spiritual obligations? It led to an underwater trip which brought the prophet to a partial recovery of his senses.

To these facets of the outer world, yet another dimension must be added. There is desperate deviation in that world. It is a rebellious world and we are in it, but not of it. Paul described it as "the domain of darkness" (Col. 1:13, NASB). Its inhabitants wallow in its shadowy pleasures. The result is cataloged in the tragic inventory of defilement described in Colossians 3:5-9. That outer world is populated with "children of disobedience" who delight to displease the Lord, consciously or otherwise.

The Christian, as he picks his way through this outer world, is always battling to maintain moral equilibrium. He seeks to be a witness while attempting to keep the wolf of humanism from devouring him and negating his God-given objectives in that world.

The second world in which believers move is the church world. This world should be fulfilling, yet so often is frustrating. It is a world of people, a strange collection of sinners-turned-saints, at least on paper. The local church is ever the measure of its individual members. Therefore, to deride the church is to deride ourselves.

Yet as we step from the outer world into the church world, we find it stifled by organization. Mini-organizations engulf us in religious busywork and institutional self-perpetuation rather than supplying a base for fellowship and evangelism. The need for structure is unquestioned, but too often it becomes an octopus, squeezing spiritual life from us. Frictions develop as pastor and people take turns creating empires within the church.

Again Paul had answers for us as he addressed the problem of suffering in the Church (Col. 1:24). This verse dealt with persecution, yet also encompassed suffering within the church. He acknowledged family bickering but admonished, "bearing with one another, and forgiving each other, whoever has a complaint against any one; just as the Lord forgave you, so also should you" (Col. 3:12-13, NASB). The eye salve of love will not blind us to our mutual failures, but it will correct our vision to the point where we can communicate with one another.

Life in the church can prove extremely tedious

without another Pauline perspective. In Colossians 1:15, 18 and 2:19 the apostle underscored the importance of cooperative effort. First, Christ is God the Sovereign; secondly, Christ is the Head of the Church; and finally, as the Church in practice becomes what it is in position, it will grow "with a growth which is from God."

Without downplaying the thrill of true church growth in these days, isn't there an increasing danger that we are becoming man-oriented? Success seems more geared to the human, than the divine personality. Apply so and so's formula and, presto, success! Is the Holy Spirit really necessary when modern methods are blazing the trail? So much of this 'success' focuses on radiant personalities, while the alarming fact is that the products in the pews often do not bear the divine good churchkeeping seal of approval.

Dr. A. W. Tozer minced no words when he wrote in this regard: "The glowworm has taken the place of the bush that burned and scintillating personalities now answer to the fire that fell at Pentecost. The fact is that we are not today producing saints. The average so-called Bible Christian in our times is but a wretched parody on true sainthood."[1]

Paul re-called the Colossians to basics, not theatrics, and challenged them to allow the peace of Christ to control their lives, a peace generated by the sustaining ministry of the Spirit through the Word. Then there would be the kind of instruction, music, and thanksgiving which would turn

31

rocky ecclesiastical groups into spiritual symphonies.

As individuals work through their relationship to the Lord, they will also begin working out their relationship with the brethren. Maybe then we will stop the flow of turned-off Christians and church-hoppers who seek some religious Shangri-La which their own lives and conduct would but adversely affect.

There is a third world in which the saint spends a portion of his hours. In fact, it is the most important world of all. It is the inner world. Buffeted by the outer world and baffled by the church world, the believer must find strength in this inner world. Here he sinks or swims, and here is determined how he will function in the other two worlds. There is the inner world of our homes. Paul dealt with this in a compact context, Colossians 3:18-21. He touched on the key characters and characteristics to be found in the Christian home. The apostle did not burden us with fancy, psychological jargon, just hard-nosed, though softhearted wisdom. Wives, husbands, children, fathers—hear ye, hear ye! Be submissive (in the Lord), be loving, be obedient, and be encouraging! Our Christian bookstores are loaded with thousands of pages on marriage, yet none can improve on Paul's simple Magna Carta for the home.

What devastation we find in homes today! As a pastor I have visited a multitude of homes, many of them plushly decorated. Yet in these same homes there is so much strife and sadness, much of it to be laid at the feet of the man of the house. Indeed the husband sets the tone in the home, and most husbands need a refresher course in loving their wives and encouraging their children.

Christian men are failing in the outer world, the church world, and the inner world of their homes because they are failing in the inner world of their hearts. Men have expended their energies in the realm of the temporal and have abdicated their responsibilities in the area of the eternal. Let us stop bewailing the place of women in the church. Christian men have created a vacuum which women have often had to fill. We should be thankful that God has used women in places where men have been conspicuous by their absence.

The solution for men, women, and youth is to be found in the nourishment of our inner lives, that world we share only with the Lord. Finding Christ has given us a good beginning (Col. 1:6), and we are to continue on from this gracious entrance into spiritual life. Paul advised us how: "As you therefore have received Christ Jesus the Lord, so walk in Him, having been firmly rooted and now being built up in Him and established in your faith. . ." (Col. 2:6-7, NASB).

At this point we come near to stepping into a dreamy world of religious clichés. The path back to basics must be trod, for the tangents of meeting-itis and experience-itis have not done the job for our generation. Personal devotional life must be reemphasized to provide that inner resiliency Christians must have. Such then offers the divine vehicle for the sponaneity and vitality churches must have and which fierce programming can never supply.

Do we wonder that our churches are filled with budding tyrants and jaded saints? We do not see in one another the very elementary evidences of the new life we are constantly chattering about in meetings. We have become cynical and burned out because we have not won the battle in our own souls. I contend that the issue is volitional. As we must will to diet, so we must prayerfully will to do God's will. Certainly our Lord conveyed the thought that growth in doctrine and life converged with a willingness to obey (John 7:17).

As we choose to follow and begin to win the inner struggle of the will, we return to the outer world with a new perspective, a concern for the lost (Col. 4:5). Then we go back to the church world with a new power, a divinely rational drive to know and serve the Lord (Ps. 42 and Ps. 84). In neither world shall we be guilty of a bizarre conduct which would alienate. We shall be real people, living a total life but with the mark of authenticity our world desperately needs to see.

Yes, our life is the Tale of Three Worlds. It will take time to unlearn much from the past. A year spent in Japan brought to my attention trees gently bent from years of pressure from the wind. So we must know the Word and allow the wind of the Spirit to bend our wills toward what a saint of

the past called "the magnetic north of the soul."
What we are in the outer and church worlds will
always be a reflection of what we are in the inner
world of our hearts.

---

1. A. W. Tozer, *Of God and Men* (Harrisburg: Christian Publications, Inc., 1960), p. 13.

5

Principles and People

When we live in an age in which the weeks pass with explosive quickness, and the months seem to collide in their race toward another January, and when life tends to dissolve into bland existence, we need to stop periodically to get our bearings. For the Christian, the Book of Second Timothy is an excellent place to enter a temporary holding pattern. It is Paul's last will and testament to the Church. Anytime someone knowingly stands in that brief interlude between time and eternity and then speaks, one does well to heed his words.

In a biographical sense 2 Timothy 4:6 is the theme of the epistle. Death was imminent for the apostle as he experienced the limitations of his final imprisonment. He was about to be offered as a living sacrifice for Christ. What did he set down as his priorities in such a situation? He reaffirmed that fine balance displayed in his ministry, the key factors of principles and people. Such a balance is still significant in the life and ministry of the church. Press the first too far, and one becomes a hide-bound legalist. Press the other, and he falls into social do-goodism. These are still the crucial areas of concern for the Church today—principles and people.

Paul always saw principles as constituting the great issues of life. What were some of those basic principles which guided his ministry? The Scriptures, of course, constituted the bedrock principle. In 2 Timothy 3:14-15 Paul reminded Timothy of his godly heritage in Lois and Eunice. They had instructed him in the truths of the Old Testament. How interesting that Paul should emphasize the redemption message from the Old Testament.

The apostle then cited that *locus classicus* of the doctrine of inspiration in the same context, verses 16-17. "All Scripture is God-breathed!" (NIV). That is the thrust of the words found at the beginning of verse 16—"God-breathed." How final and assuring! What sadness that much learning has made some modern-day disciples mad enough to lead them to question the authority of Scriptures. As God pronounced His benediction on other creative activity, so He has done the same for the Scriptures. Because of His very nature, one could not expect from God anything less than inerrancy in the autographs. Though using human agency to write, and not reducing the writing role to mere dictation, God still bequeathed to man an inerrant revelation of His truth in written form. The powerful writings stir men from the sleep of sin and death as the Holy Spirit employs His sword to slice away the webs of darkness and unbelief and then produces new birth life.

From this beginning the child of God then gleans instruction through the Word as he moves ahead into a life of maturity characterized by good works, "spiritual works of art" as Paul called them in Ephesians 2:10.

Another principle which surfaces in this epistle deals with the cataclysmic events of the future. Paul referred to the convulsive last days of human civilization in 2 Timothy 3:1-5. What stands out about these grievous last days is the self-centered drift of life, accompanied by powerful forces of deception. No doubt there was a foretaste of this in the first century. Only once in the New Testament is the expression *self-lovers* used, and that in verse two of this context.

The variety of terms Paul used described a society going berserk, with a disruption of the most elemental of value systems. The primacy of self is uppermost. I recall days of basic training in the army. While in the field on training exercises, we were totally dependent for our food on the trucks which came out from camp. If you were at the end of the chow line, so often you would be taunted by those passing with filled mess kits, "I got my share. How are you doing?" That is rapidly becoming the philosophy of modern man. If people were shot in gasoline lines, what will happen when they have to stand in food lines?

The thirteenth verse of this chapter underscores another malady of the last days—deception. In modern terms Paul would say that swindlers, and manipulators of the truth will abound. Jesus warned of the same in His Olivet discourse. Jonestown has to be the still incredible ultimate of deception, when people were swindled out of their very lives.

In contradistinction Paul offered another principle. There are eternal standards no matter what the passing whims of time may bring to any generation. Such standards are described at the outset of 2 Timothy 4. Though people crave novel allurements, still the Word must be preached. The sheep must receive the marvelous diet of manna week in and week out.

It is somewhat alarming to discover a growing biblical illiteracy in the church. With all the multiple Bible translations and study aids, we still face congregations more familiar with batting averages than the books of the Bible. There remains that painful, yet essential, apprenticeship which must be experienced to master the Word, that the Word might master us.

The word translated "sound" throughout the pastoral epistles is a medical term which means "to set a broken bone." The application spiritually is obvious, and such is achieved as sound doctrine is inculcated in the believer. As if to urge Timothy to keep his own house in order, the apostle admonished him to concentrate on his relationship to the Lord and to accomplish the unique task entrusted to him.

A fourth principle elaborated upon by Paul resided in the concept of security. This is expressed in 2 Timothy 1:12. Paul could face death with assurance. He had absolute confidence in the gospel. Therefore he committed, as a sacred deposit, his life, his soul, his ministry to the Lord. Without shame or reservation, Paul could do this!

What a tremendous source of strength and motivation such hope constitutes—to know that life has real purpose and that all of these life-transforming principles are indeed rooted in the sovereign Son of God (2 Tim. 1:9-10).

But now we turn to the other side of the coin of life in Paul's set of priorities. If principles are the great issues, then people are the great issue. I once heard someone say, "Get mad at me, say what you want to me, but please don't ignore me." A frenzied, restless age has left a depersonalized litter of humanity on the beaches of society. Does it sound strange to hear that our churches have also created hosts of ignored people? Are we so pre-occupied with size and activity that we are failing to be concerned about people?

As Paul concluded this his final epistle, should he not have given some new theological insights? But he "disappoints" us by leaving a catalog of names, the names of ordinary people. What a strange climax to a great writing career. But these made up the stuff of the apostle's life and ministry. There were all kinds of people mentioned in this letter.

Paul mentioned helping people such as Timothy (2 Tim. 1:2), his spiritually begotten son in the faith. There were the aforementioned Lois and Eunice (2 Tim. 1:5), who overcame a divided household to share Christ with others. There was also the gracious Onesiphorus, who ministered to Paul in seasons of need and loneliness (2 Tim. 1:16-18).

However, people come in all shapes and varieties. Paul also had encountered hindering people. His day also had its share of unreliables. People such as Phygellus and Hermogenes (2 Tim. 1:15) had set Paul adrift in some still unknown fashion. Others hindered by espousing false teaching, witness Hymenaeus and Philetus (2 Tim. 2:16-18). Times have not changed as pastors and people still struggle with the inroads of arrogant artisans of error. And there was an Alexander (2 Tim. 4:14-15). Paul had been wounded in spiritual conflict with this individual. I like the human touch seen in, "The Lord reward him according to his works." Perhaps, in the heat of the occasion, Paul might have desired fire to descend on, or the earth to open for Alexander, but he kept it to himself. Yes, there were those who had caused the apostle much grief.

In reflecting upon the years, this faithful servant of God recalled that there were also hurting people. There were the spiritually sick such as Demas (2 Tim. 4:10a). Demas was no flash-in-the-pan follower of the Way. In Colossians and Philemon Paul used his name in close association with Luke's. Yet there was a gnawing illness in Demas, a disease not totally rooted out—"having loved this present world [age]." How ironic, Demas deserted Paul because he loved the now-world at the very time Paul anticipated entering the next world.

Positively, there were people hurting for the cause of Christ, such as Trophimus (2 Tim. 4:20b). Casualties had been sustained in the cause of preaching the gospel. There will continue to be casualties in the days to come. We must be willing to accept that fact. Not everyone we work with will come through for the Lord. Some will be seduced by false teaching, and others will endure lives of suffering beyond our ability to understand.

As Paul neared the end of this epistle, he again thought of helping people (2 Tim. 4:11-13, 19-21). Could we call them the Honor Roll of the Anonymous? These names stand for real people—people we shall meet in heaven one day! These are the unknowns who keep churches and missions going by their loyal commitment to Christ. Their names would not be recorded today in the religious journals, nor would they be identified with the elite who dazzle congregations and conferences. But they are the real sinew of the church whose presence and practice ensures continuity.

Is it not the supreme measure of the apostle's life that he chose to end this letter, so fraught with trauma for him, with a list of believers? Why? Because these people were the individuals he had come to love and for whom Christ had died. People constituted the great issue of life. Conversely, as he faced death, Paul set forth the great issues, the principles of truth on which his life had been based.

As we seek to pull our lives together in muddled and confused times, as we contemplate our personal anticipation of 2 Timothy 4:6, we need to maintain a precious, yet ever precarious balance. Such a balance will find us moving in a sphere of ministry centered on a principles/people rotation. How the church needs to hold fast to that holy focus which constantly relates truth to people!

6

The Lost Treasure

We observe annually special occasions in the life of the church. Christmas, Easter, and Pentecost are ones which immediately come to mind. But whatever we called it, we would not be far afield to schedule a yearly sermon entitled, "Lost in Church—One Bible." Everyone should remember the text from Sunday school days, 2 Kings 22:8, "I have found the book of the law in the house of the Lord." Hilkiah, the high priest, was the speaker.

And where else would you expect to find the book of the law? Church people today could identify with such a happening. Don't they lose coats, hats, umbrellas, consciousness, even Bibles in church? Check the lost and found department of most churches, and you will find enough Bibles to start a new denomination.

For an individual to leave his Bible in church, even for weeks, is one matter, but for an entire nation to lose the Word of God in the house of God for decades is quite another. New Englanders can appreciate the enormity of such an occurrence. In their region, spiritual awakening swept the countryside in colonial times and made a great impact on society. At one time even voting privileges were linked to good standing in an orthodox church. Now that early Bible belt region has exchanged its loyalty to the gospel for secular humanism.

Church history and the Old Testament do reveal that, impossible as it seems, the Bible can be lost in the very place it should be treasured and taught. The danger today resides in the variety of sub rosa influences permeating the pulpits and programs of churches. These have a biblical veneer without a biblical veracity. Bad enough that men "strut and fret" before congregations, but worse still that we are being treated to psychological and methodological emphases which skim over the needy nerve endings of believers. Woe to the modern Jeremiah who would dare challenge "the peace, peace" of the prophets of religious technology!

So a "Lost in Church—One Bible" Sunday might well remind us annually of the importance of preserving biblical exposition. The passage in 2 Kings 22 does reveal a pattern for the constant discovery and dissemination of the Word of God. First, there was concern on the part of a man. That man was King Josiah. Although ascending the throne of Judah as a mere youth, he received this later evaluation, "He did that which was right in the sight of the Lord" (2 Kings 22:2).

In a way there never should have been a Josiah. His grandfather was the wicked Manasseh who ruled for fifty-five years; his father, the weak Amon, added another two years because he "forsook the Lord God of his fathers, and walked not in the way of the Lord" (2 Kings 21:22). Still, it is comforting to realize that God did intervene and introduced new life into a line which had produced spiritual death for decades.

At the age of eighteen the young king began to assume leadership. He had become sensitive to the insensitivity of his people, spawned by a lack of systematic teaching of the law. Josiah had a burden for the house of God. He did not perceive the full implications of this concern, but he started where he could. His concern produced a growing concern among others. There is a need for people today with concern that will look to God for direction in ministry. So often the spontaneous outflow of the Spirit seems shut off while bedazzled laymen wait for the experts to come and tell them how and what to do.

What a spring of life came from Josiah's burden! A scribe, the high priest, carpenters, builders, and stone masons were caught up in the drama. From that mundane matter of temple repair something wonderful developed. We follow the trail and discover that from this concern came a cleansing of sin. Knowing something of the character of Manasseh, one could believe that early in his reign the teaching of the law had been muzzled until finally it was lost in the shuffle of idolatrous practices. Easily half a century had elapsed without the convicting call of the Word. Then Shaphan the scribe read to the king from the newly recovered law.

The young king responded in a very unkingly way. He began to tear his clothes, even as the truth tore at his heart. In innocent ignorance he had been ruling without clear directives from his King. Second Kings 22:13 summarizes Josiah's concern: "Go ye, inquire of the Lord for me, and for the people, and for all Judah, concerning the words of this book that is found: for great is the wrath of the Lord that is kindled against us, because our fathers have not hearkened unto the words of this book, to do according to all that which is written concerning us."

Then, with the aid of Huldah the prophetess, truth was once more declared from the law, and this commendation came to Josiah, "Because thine heart was tender, and thou hast humbled thyself before the Lord. . .and hast rent thy clothes, and wept before me; I also have heard thee, saith the Lord" (2 Kings 22:19).

An amazing chain reaction came about because a young man was concerned about the Lord's honor, especially as manifest in the condition of His house. An interesting sidelight is the fact that Josiah wept. One has to wonder if the lachrymal gland will become as vestigial an organ as the appendix is thought to be, useless because it is not used. Our churches need a bathing in tears, not from mere emotion, but from Spirit-induced conviction. We are stoic and unmoved by our sins and the lost condition of those about us. How refreshing to read that Josiah wept.

His tears were the prelude to decisive action.

Then followed the fruit of biblical repentance. King Josiah sensed the urgency of relating this graciously awesome news to his people. He gathered about him in the temple environs the leaders and citizens of Jerusalem and Judah (2 Kings 23:1-2). He personally read "in their ears all the words of the book of the covenant."

Josiah then instituted a sweeping campaign against the multiplicity of evils which had swept the nation, the city, and the temple itself. Almost beyond belief is the list of a frightening variety of sins which had gripped a nation through which the Messiah was destined to come. One detects a similar breakdown among believers today. Divorce, infidelity, careless living, uncommitted wills, and raw materialism compose that catalog of sins which have smitten Christians today. One needs a scorecard to tell the saints from the sinners. Then we read that Josiah, "brake down the houses of the sodomites, that were by the house of the Lord" (2 Kings 23:7). Need comment even be made about the nauseous acceptance of the unacceptable in the visible church of our times?

Negative action alone was not enough. From the cleansing produced by the concern, there sprang a fresh commitment to the Lord. Although some question the abiding impact of Josiah's reformation, still it was an oasis in a desert of spiritual dereliction. Thus the words, "And the king stood. . .and made a covenant before the Lord. . . and all the people stood to the covenant" (2 Kings

23:3). What a glorious event in the light of the previous chaos under Manasseh and Amon!

Sorrow turned to song as Josiah called those present to observe the nation's birthday. Passover was indeed this nation's day of independence. For a brief season, rays of truth shone brightly between a grim past and an uncertain future, "surely there was not holden such a passover from the days of the judges. . ." (2 Kings 23:22). The nation recalled that time when God had torn a son from the matrix of Goshen to establish a new hope in the land of promise.

But the continued need for cleansing described in this chapter bespeaks how deeply evil had attached itself to the moral fiber of the people. They were even involved with familiar spirits and wizards. Practioners of the occult had woven their deluding web over the life of this nation. Though one rejoices in what proved to be a stay of execution, still the inevitability of divine judgment was clear.

The account reveals that rediscovery of God's Word brought renewal. But we must be aware of the Jerusalem captivity which preceded the Babylonian captivity. Adding up the years of Manasseh, Amon, and the beginning of Josiah's reign gives us some seventy years when a nation of the Book lived without the Book. Does this seem unrelated to the present? Can "Lost in Church— One Bible" be relevant in a day when translations proliferate and Bible study materials pour off the presses? The Word was available at the beginning of the Jerusalem captivity. But it became fashionable to avoid the truth or to be conscious of truth, but not to live the truth. The obvious conclusion is that the treasure of the Word was lost by degrees. An entire nation became dull of hearing because it failed to obey what it had heard.

Could this be happening in our churches? First, one wonders if the sheep in the pews are actually being fed. Plugs for programs and personalities plus stories and hoopla have invaded many a pulpit. How much real biblical content could be distilled from the typical evangelical sermon today? Dr. A. W. Tozer warned of this danger years ago when he wrote: "The great god Entertainment amuses his devotees mainly by telling them stories. The love of stories, which is a characteristic of childhood, has taken fast hold of the minds of the retarded saints of our day. . . What is natural and beautiful in a child may be shocking when it persists into adulthood, and more so when it appears in the sanctuary and seeks to pass for true religion."[1]

Dr. Tozer contended for a spiritual environment which blended truth with the Spirit of Truth in such a way that Christ was exalted and man kept in his proper place. Otherwise, if the roles are reversed, we become dull after years of listening. Churches are then populated with believers who are satiated and stagnant after a lifetime of listening and who have never crawled out of their cribs into spiritual adulthood. Fault lies both in the pulpits and in the pews.

Equally serious is the danger of the experiencism which stalks our sanctuaries as many look for a religious fix which will send them sky-high, yet keep them removed from the reality of living a godly life in a workaday world.

History gives many examples of nations, cities, and regions once blessed of God and now spiritually barren. North Africa, in apostolic time, was evangelized and a strong church emerged. Now that region is one of the most difficult mission fields in the world. New England was the center of the great spiritual awakening in the colonial period but is now largely unresponsive to gospel truth.

Judah, before Josiah, North Africa and New England warn us that truth can be lost in the temple. Continual concern, cleansing, and commitment alone will enable us to retain that precious treasure, the Word of God. Let us not lose what so many desperately need to find!

We have considered some of the basic principles necessary for maintaining biblical practice in the life of the church, but we do well to pause at this juncture to focus on a vital, yet oftentimes neglected facet of truth.

The vertical must constantly intersect the horizontal, that is, the Divine must ever touch the human to continue true perspective and real power. Otherwise we become too smart for our own spiritual welfare, and too busy to cultivate the friendship of God.

For to love and to worship God in the Spirit,

one must also do the same in truth. There are some truths about God which are not frequently considered these days. The themes which now follow seek to reaffirm important truths for us to hold to that we may cleave to a divine perspective in the ongoing experience of the Church.

1. A. W. Tozer, *The Best of A. W. Tozer*, comp. Warren Wiersbe (Harrisburg: Christian Publications, Inc., 1978), p. 128.

II. Seeking

7

The Anguish of God

Although numerous hurricanes have ravaged New England through the years, one in particular seems to come to the fore in conversation with old-timers. That is the hurricane of 1938. I was just a boy at the time, but can still remember standing on our front porch, awed by the gusting winds and frightened by the inundating floods of water driven inland from Long Island Sound. Days later, as some normality returned, an excursion to the shoreline areas revealed ancient trees uprooted and pleasure craft scattered across the beaches.

I have been told that at the center of each hurricane there is an eye that is a place of calm. Air Force weather planes have verified this fact. Thus in the midst of natural turbulence there is a place of relative safety and calm. For centuries mankind has looked back to a spiritual hurricane. A fury, never before envisioned by man, engulfed a man, the God-man. It swirled about Him and sought to overcome Him in a cascade of sin and shame. Yet in the midst of that hurricane, there was a calm. One person retained His dignity surrounded by a crowd gone berserk for blood. Jesus Christ hung on a cross; yet He, not the crucifiers, was in command. The eye, the peace of doing only the will of the Father, was underscored by those words of reigning resignation, "Father, into thy hands I commend my spirit" (Luke 23:46).

We do well to consider the hurricane and the calm of Calvary. In them we discover two aspects of this hurricane force let loose because of the Savior's life and ministry. There was first the human side. What magnificent self-control the Lord demonstrated when He was accosted by Judas and that band of official brigands (Matt. 26:47). How bizarre to see a people committed to law espousing such lawlessness. They came to seize an individual known for His honoring of the law. All of this was but a part of Satan's insidious web to entrap and neutralize the Savior.

Though one of His own sought to meet the enemy on its terms with violence, the Lord rebuked that conduct and healed the injury caused by the same (Luke 22:50-51). How we need to recognize that the Lord's way will run counter to trying to match swords with the world on its own turf.

The hellish force of this human hurricane continued and swept Jesus into the presence of the community's lawkeepers. Their conduct seems almost irrational as compared to their normal standards of fair play, but such was easily dismissed by their manic desire to eliminate this threat to the status quo.

Biblical scholars have detailed the numerous illegal acts committed against the Son of Man by these protectors of orthodoxy. What stands out is the venom released against Him (Matt. 26:65-67). Such are the deeds of a mob, not at all in keeping with the temperate conduct expected of the Sanhedrin. Especially vicious was their disregard for the sanctity of life. It stemmed from their covetous desire to maintain an already tenuous control beneath the yoke of Roman authority. Such egocentric thinking veiled their minds from seeing the fulfillment of their Messianic dreams standing incarnate in their presence.

It must have been a wild scene described for us by Matthew (27:19-20). Pilate, filled with foreboding by his wife's warnings, was now a ruler being ruled by circumstances beyond his control. History will always portray Pilate's weakness in the washing of his hands. His final destiny was tragic, concluded in disgrace. Yet, I sense that Pilate saw something in Christ, the first genuine person he had met in a lifetime of surveying a gallery of religious charlatans. Still, Pilate allowed his own conduct to lock him into an inevitable decision. He now had to reap what he had sown. One does not undercut confidence in the power of the gospel to recognize that some people repeat the error of Pilate, and that they, too, seek to wash away their guilt with the waters of self-vindication, rather than with the blood of Christ.

Little did those present realize how completely their words would return when, in response to Pilate they shouted, "His blood be on us, and on our children" (Matt. 27:24-25). Titus Vespasian would squeeze the very last drop from their vindicative outcry when he razed Jerusalem in A.D. 70.

The force of that human hurricane peaked as the Romans led Christ to Calvary. Whipped up by agitators, the atmosphere was one of a grisly carnival. The Sanhedrin, delirious over their victory, exchanged knowing nods, for Pilate had become their pawn in dealing with this dangerous Nazarene. The street-hawkers plied their trade while this judicial farce was played out in the alleys of Jerusalem. Violence, hatred, deception, and soon death all exploded on the now weakened and sorrowful Savior.

It was no pleasant sight as He trod the Via Dolorosa, for it was a pain-filled pilgrimage prompted by our sin. Then the human tempest began to expend itself with the simple and awful words, "And they crucified him" (Matt. 27:35).

But as this human fury subsided, another took hold. The Father had eternally purposed this moment in order that fallen creatures could have paradise regained. Yet, there is the feel of divine restraint in the use of His power as if the Father had said, "I allow my Son's death, but see what a perilous path you tread in crucifying Him." He manifested His restrained power in a series of supernatural events.

First there was the unnatural darkness which swirled down on the land for some three hours. We always think of God in terms of light, yet there are divine darknesses such as this which trouble and perplex. One thinks of the intense darkness of

Passover night as the death angel gathered his harvest in Egypt, and now the death angel faced that inexplicable task in the expiration of Jesus Christ, who died to "taste death for every man" (Heb. 2:9).

What were people thinking about in those baffling hours of blackness? At least nature expressed its shame at the events on earth. Those present must have realized that more was on the way—that God would release further manifestations of His holy displeasure. As one feels thick darkness before the unleashing of a tornado, so here darkness ushered in new acts of power.

We read of this in Matthew 27:51, "And, behold, the veil of the temple was rent in twain from the top to the bottom." This had to be amazing to those priests on duty, for it took place at the time of preparation for the evening sacrifice. No infidel had entered the temple and by human hands cut this heavy curtain from bottom to top. But divine power accomplished this, and now priests other than the high priests gazed into the most holy place for the first time, and lived!

The writer of Hebrews interpreted the above for us in chapter 10:19-20, "Having therefore, brethren, boldness to enter into the holiest by the blood of Jesus, by a new and living way, which he hath consecrated for us, through the veil, that is to say, his flesh. . . ." He who had seen the Son had seen the Father, and now the way was open wide to all who repented and believed. One wonders at the relationship of the rending of the veil and the words in Acts 6:7, "A great company of the priests were obedient to the faith." Surely the impact of the veil's being rent was used to turn many to the Great High Priest. Now all had direct access to God through the Son.

How were the religious leaders responding to all of this? As these strange reports filtered back, they must have felt their control of affairs slowly slipping away.

"And the earth did quake, and the rocks rent" (Matt. 27:51). I recall standing at the end of a very substantial dock in Yokohama, Japan, when an earth tremor struck. That dock began to quiver as if it were rubber. I remember my reaction—running toward the land end of the dock! Earthquakes do not go unnoticed!

Not only the events themselves—darkness, rent veil, earthquake—but the timing must have also created an uneasiness in the people of Jerusalem. Was not the well-advertised event of the Nazarene's crucifixion taking place on this day? God had withheld His power to allow the crucifixion, but He would not allow business as usual on this day without etching some sharp lessons in human minds.

The most significant phase of the divine hurricane was yet to come. Matthew 27:52-53 describes it. There was a shaking of the world to come. Witnesses had now to contend with literal resurrection. "If a man die, shall he live again?" (Job 14:14). After the Lord's resurrection, the Scriptures report, "saints...came out of the graves

. . .and went into the holy city, and appeared unto many." What possible explanations could cover the impossible? What happened to these individuals later? Their appearance either softened countless hearts or else prompted a complete closure to God's workings.

As these human and divine forces whirled around the cross, what of the one who hung on that cross? In the midst of it all there came the most awesome occurrence of all. Such was centered in the mysterious and impenetrable words, "My God, my God, why hast thou forsaken me?" (Matt. 27:46). One steps back in bewilderment at those words. Few have ever come near to fathoming their meaning. One surmises that the bearing of man's sin had created a rift never before experienced in the Godhead.

Such words as "he himself bore our sins in his body on the tree" (1 Pet. 2:24, NIV) and "he hath made him to be sin for us, who knew no sin" (2 Cor. 5:21) help slightly to grasp something of the magnitude of this forsaking. That sickening mass of the sins of the human race was in some fashion affixed to the sinless Lamb of God. Why, though not how, we understand. He was our substitute, and for that fleeting instant the Father was repulsed from the presence of the Son by the presence of sin. On such holy ground we can but kick off the sandals of our minds and stand in silence. This necessary forsaking of the Son produced the anguish of God anticipated from the trackless ages of eternity.

Yet even in this, there was an eye in the hurricane, truly a calm within the storm. For from that place of physical and spiritual agony came words which revealed a tested person totally under control. Whereas most of us would have called for avenging lightning, He said, "Father, forgive them; for they know not what they do" (Luke 23:34).

Forgive the crucifiers? That's not the norm for us. We who would excoriate an errant motorist on the highway are not given to such forgiveness. And what of his concern for the welfare of those on crosses beside Him? In the press of such agony He was still able to offer hope and redemption to one who trusted Him at the very last instant.

The drama built again until out of this boiling caldron of forces a shout was heard, a great cry, and one word, "Finished!" John gave us that information (John 19:30). It was a shout, not of torment, but of triumph. He had drunk to the final drop of the judgment for man's sin, and then of the wrath of God against that sin. And now He, the Eternal One, must taste death for every man.

Not the exhaustion of crucifixion, but rather a willing submission, brought the pangs of death upon Him. "Finished!" That shouted word bridged His inmost being and the outer world. He had now pleased the Father by accomplishing the Father's will.

Then another word issued from that place of peace. "Father, into thy hands I commend my spirit" (Luke 23:46). Actually, this was a prayer, a quotation of Psalm 31:5 with the addition of the word, "Father." These words were drawn from the experience of the lesser David as in affliction from Saul he faced the possibility of death.

We are told that this is the first prayer a Jewish mother taught her child, similar to our own, "Now I lay me down to sleep." The child would repeat these words at bedtime. How well said, "Even on the cross Jesus died as a child falling asleep—in His Father's arms." There was a holy serenity as the Son faced death. Here was the ultimate commitment, a volitional act of trust in the face of man's most feared enemy.

The force of the hurricane had expended itself on the Lord, but now it swept past Him and produced shock waves in those about the cross. A hardened professional soldier was turned from the inglorious task of an execution to the glorious trust of a worshipper (Luke 23:47). Whereas Pilate had sidestepped the implications of this unique life, the centurion surrendered and confessed, "Certainly, this was a righteous man!"

Others gave way to confusion, anger, and frustration, vaguely aware that something heinous had been inflicted on an innocent and remarkable person, yet unable to acknowledge their guilt and need (Luke 23:48).

We need not beat our breasts in hopeless resignation. We know who He is and why He died on that cross. In the hurricane forces of modern life, we are asked to trust Him as Savior and then serve Him with our lives. Only then can we, in the midst of explosive change, find the eye of the hurricane, the calm of God, that peace which the world cannot give.

Thus in quiet confidence we can appreciate afresh the majestic control of the Son as we also recognize the anguish of the Father. Then we, His blood-bought children, can whisper, "Father, into Thy hands I commit my life. You do with it what is best for You, for that will be eternally good for me."

8

The Anger of God

"It is my opinion that the Christian conception of God currently in vogue in these middle years of the twentieth century is so decadent as to be utterly beneath the dignity of the Most High God and actually to constitute for professed believers something amounting to a moral calamity."[1] These incisive words of Dr. A. W. Tozer still ring true, though that choice servant of the Lord is no longer with us. The intervening years since his departure have not changed the downward spiral. If anything, the pace has accelerated.

Dr. Tozer targeted these words beyond the merely religious world to the evangelical world. It is disturbing to conjecture whether the Lord is really needed today in some churches. High voltage personalities who roam the pulpits, directing wide-ranging programs staffed with multitudes of professionals and powered by up-to-date methodology, prompt the question. It seems to be man's turn at bat in the church.

The electronic church especially fosters this image of man in control, gathering partisan followers who speak of "so and so's ministry or church," not God's. To speed the processing of followers, simplistic solutions are tendered. Thus many become busy chanting the litany of easy steps to God while forgetting, or never knowing, who God really is. Television theology now sits comfortably on the tray with TV dinners, both easily prepared and just as easily dispensed with.

But I have long been intrigued with that "other side of God," that which Luther called "the strange work of God." It is the side of God no one mentions any more, unless it is done with dispatch by relating the subject to Old Testament times. Paul told the Ephesians to be "angry, and sin not" (Eph. 4:26). Does anger also have a place in the activities of Deity?

Recall that perplexing incident in 2 Samuel 6. David was returning the ark of God to Jerusalem. It was a happy occasion, marking hopes for a bright new future for the nation. A man named Uzzah was one of those entrusted with driving the specially made cart containing the ark. As they advanced, the cart passed over a threshing floor. For some reason the oxen started to stumble, and as they did, Uzzah did what most of us would have done. He reached out to steady the ark to keep it from falling.

And what happened? "The anger of the Lord was kindled against Uzzah; and God smote him there for his error [rashness]; and there he died by the ark of God" (2 Sam. 6:7). I admit to not understanding this, and all the commentators I have read have yet to satisfy me on this incident. Apparently it was also a dilemma for David, for we read, "Then David was angry because the

Lord's wrath had broken out against Uzzah" (2 Sam. 6:8, NIV).

Perhaps Uzzah was wrongly motivated as he proudly drove the cart and then presumptuously sought "to help God" by steadying the ark. But then the answer may reside in the idea of doing the right thing the wrong way, of allowing mere human enthusiasm to intrude into areas not so intended by God. In reading Numbers 4, one discovers a very detailed pattern for transporting the ark. Only Levites were to bear the ark on their shoulders, and the selfsame Levites were not to touch the ark on penalty of death.

Familiarity had bred contempt for holy things. Years before, the Israelites had used the ark of God as a good luck charm in battle against the Philistines, and they had been decisively trounced. This visible reminder of the presence of God was not to be used as a magic amulet, and neither can a lot of modern methodology in the church today. But I do feel for Uzzah, for I think I would have done the same thing, and by saying these words, I recognize that familiarity does breed contempt.

Several years ago I was in the Boston area, thumbing through a local newspaper (working my way back to the only rational section—the sports page), when these words caught my eye, "Electrician electrocuted in downtown store." Now of all people who should not be electrocuted, electricians should be the ones. The paper's account of the incident did not spell out the details, but I wondered at the time whether the individual had grown careless with something which proved to be fatally familiar for him.

That can also happen to those of us who are in constant touch with the things of God, and may provide a good reason why we should give more thought these days to the anger of God. I reject the deistic view of God which leaves Him way off somewhere with no personal interest in man, but then I also reject a modern day syrupy familiarity with God as well.

The Old Testament is replete with illustrations of this facet of the acts of God. Think of a few of them. God was disturbed and grieved when he, "saw that the wickedness of man was great in the earth, and that every imagination of the thoughts of his heart was only evil continually" (Gen. 6:5-6). The ensuing flood was an expression of both the holiness and the righteous anger of God. Even then provision was made for redemption through a water-borne ark.

The command to annihilate the Canaanites seems difficult to balance with the idea of a loving God, yet historians have pointed to the utter degradation of that culture. Certainly the anger of God had a purgative effect. And what of the "arbitrary" treatment of the Israelites at Ai simply because Achan had sinned? Why did so many have to suffer because of the sin of one man? Then there is that awesome series of events in Numbers, chapter 16 when the earth opened and swallowed Korah with his rebellious followers, followed by the fire and plague as more were killed (Num. 16:32-50). What also of the devouring flame which extinguished the lives of Nadab and Abihu, the sons of Aaron, for offering strange fire before the Lord (Lev. 10:1-2)? These are but a few of the many manifestations of the visible anger of God against both the pagan and His people. Indeed, we agree with Luther, "This is the strange work of God."

But then the "strangest" of all was His treatment of Israel and Judah, surrendering them to the swords of Assyria and then Babylon. What an insulting thing it is to walk out of a person's presence in seething anger! Yet Jehovah went step-by-step out of the most holy place and from the jewel of His eye, Jerusalem, when He departed from His people. Ezekiel sadly described that progression of the departure of the presence of God (Ezek. 10:4-18). The exiles knew then that there would be no quick return from captivity. And was not that the ultimate expression of divine anger against a nation, His nation, which had sinned and rebelled?

Even in the citing of these Old Testament incidents, we detect an encompassing grace and goodness of God. Promises of restoration and future blessing dot the countryside of prophetic writings. We speak here with a groping anthropomorphism about God and His anger. It is an anger long held in restraint. It is not irrational, spur-of-the-moment anger, as is ours. When related to His people, it is an anger prompted by sin, especially the sin of presumption.

This presumption troubles perceptive Christians. There is today so very much of man and his means seeking to do in human energy that which only the Spirit's energy can achieve. What alerts this writer is the evidence that divine anger does not end with the Book of Malachi. God's anger in the New Testament? How can that be?

Some would concede that Paul intimated an anger of God as he wrote of "the wrath of God" in the Roman epistle and that John portrayed the same in the Apocalypse, and then would close the discussion there. But what of Ananias and Sapphira, who pretended to be what they were not? If this same standard were enforced today, all church activities would be replaced by a continual round of funeral services.

The Lord, filled with holy jealousy for His budding Church, dealt decisively with such spiritual disease in the young fellowship (Acts 5). There is also the pulse of restrained anger throughout the Corinthian letters. Satanic effort sought to subvert the light in the darkness of Corinthian chaos. In the explosive closing portion of Second Corinthians, Paul denounced the challenge to apostolic authority which was but a covert challenge to God's authority.

Next we come to those words surrounding the observance of the Lord's Supper. Surely, as the Holy of Holies in the tabernacle and temple needed to be guarded from desecration, likewise that special occasion, the Table of the Lord, required equal care. So special was this communion that many believe Paul received a distinct revelation about the table, "For I have received of the Lord that which also I delivered unto you" (1 Cor. 11:23). In the closing portion of this passage, the apostle moved into words of warning. All of us have wrestled with the meaning of "unworthily." In reading 1 Corinthians 11:30 we discover the consequences of carelessness with and at the Lord's Supper. "For this cause many are weak and sickly among you, and many sleep." Physical affliction was visited on believers for spiritual carelessness, even to the extreme of death.

Is not this an example of the anger of God? Exactly what was involved here we do not know, but this unworthy conduct precipitated unusual action by the Lord. That equally disturbing verse in 1 John 5:16 may well be appropo here, "There is a sin unto death." John was writing to believers, yet he suggested that there was some kind of disobedience by a believer which could issue in physical death.

I recall following the promising career of a prize fighter who professed openly to being a Christian. He began to move toward a championship fight in his weight division. Then I read of his death in an auto "accident." People close to the individual had detected a drifting away from the Lord as success increased, and it was their opinion that his seemingly premature death may well have been directed of the Lord. That is a precarious observation to make about anyone's life, yet mature believers felt this was true of the young fighter.

Granted, many New Testament portions (2 Peter, Jude, Revelation) speak of God's anger toward the ungodly, but dare we assign divine anger to the redeemed as well? Is not anger also intimated in the letter to the Laodiceans because they were neither hot nor cold but lukewarm, thus "I will spit you out of My mouth" (Rev. 3:16, NASB).

Our present evangelical mind set finds it difficult to square the love of God as manifest on Calvary with the ominous overtones of an angry God, Jonathan Edwards notwithstanding. Nor is it the writer's intent to lead us back into some slavish legalism which demands the placating of an angry God. Still the products of our easy believism and simplistic formulae give pause to those who wonder when the quality will catch up to the quantity in the church. Somber morbidity surely is not the hallmark of true worship of God, yet neither is the frothy, flippant attitude found in the house of God these days. We cannot rise higher than our view of God, and surely this generation's view of God demands elevation.

The classic illustration of the anger of God was revealed on two occasions in the temple by the Son of God. There was enacted a furious and violent maelstrom of emotion by the incarnate Son. What a volcanic overflow of anger was His! Why? Because the very place where men were to be brought close to God had become the very place where men were being turned away from God.

Could that be happening today in our churches? Is man so prominent that he has deflected people's attention from the eternal one who is both merciful, yet holy? Our message of grace needs a firmer backbone of theology which will reveal the nature of God and, in so doing, bring modern man to his knees in contrition and adoration.

What restraint there must be in the heavenly portals these days as mere men strut across the stage of the church and receive glory to themselves. Surely God has been angry with all of us! It may well be that the intercessory work of the Son and the Spirit at the throne of grace has spared us the consequences of our own presumption in the work of the Lord. How often have we, as Uzzah of old, put our hands on the ark of God?

Well did that experienced and wise preacher admonish: "Keep thy foot when thou goest to the house of God, and be more ready to hear, than to give the sacrifice of fools; for they consider not that they do evil" (Eccles. 5:1). The Spanish rendering brings this verse into sharper focus, "Watch your step when you go to the house of God."

Somehow, without lapsing into a phobic fear of God, we need a balanced view of the Lord which shows His mercy toward sinners, yet His firmness toward sin. We need "to watch our step" as we worship and serve Him, and not unwittingly to drag Him down to a dangerous and false familiarity which eventually will lead to contempt.

Have you struggled with me in this difficult consideration—the anger of God? Kept in balance, the truths of God are always compensatory. There is much blessing to be found in an equality between grace and justice as we observe God's anguish and anger in dealing with man.

---

1. A. W. Tozer, *The Knowledge of the Holy* (New York: Harper and Brothers, Publishers, 1961), p. 10.

9

The Awe of God

In the summer of 1969 a devastating tornado moved across the northeastern edge of Cincinnati, Ohio. A missionary who was to speak in the church the following day told us later of how he sat helpless in a restaurant, watching a funnel cloud as it swept across a busy intersection and literally sucked the roof from a building only yards from where he was.

Because it happened so quickly, he had little time to react. Later he recalled a strange feeling inside, doubtless a rising fear in the face of that powerful natural phenomenon. Fear, by its very nature, offers two options. Either it can paralyze and cripple one confronted by danger and emergency situations, or it can raise one to a pitch which results in high performance and oftentimes superhuman effort.

We increasingly see in our times the increase of both overt and suppressed fears. The preoccupation with mental health movements and jokes about psychiatrists' couches alert us to the realization that fear stalks the land. Christ related this to the end times when He spoke of, "Men's hearts failing them for fear, and for looking after those things which are coming on the earth" (Luke

21:26). This is taking place as the pressures and uncertainties of modern life constrict and paralyze the hearts of men.

Normally the concept of fear elicits negative feelings, and thus to use this word in conjunction with God creates an uneasiness. Shouldn't we love God? Is He not a God of grace and of mercy? Why should we, so far removed from Old Testament days, fear the Lord? For simply pragmatic reasons we need a return to the fear of God. Our approach to Deity is sadly lacking. Modern man has deified man and humanized God, and the church has not escaped the fallout from that kind of thinking.

One does not need to equate the fear of God with somber countenances; however, the fad of familiarity with God has not produced a generation of spiritual giants. Our music, manners, and methods have brought Him down to our level. The fact is, He remains aloof from the superficial atmosphere which pervades so much of what transpires in our churches.

Even working within the New Testament framework, one finds ample indication that the Savior must still be approached as the Sovereign. The fear of God is not easily defined. One definition speaks of "reverential trust." That is a start. But even against the shadow of the cross and the open door of access to the most holy which the writer of Hebrews set forth, the fact remains that He is the Unknown-Known One.

Because we have brought Him down to our

level, we have produced a whole series of simplistic formulae by which we think we can ascend to His level. The gospel message is essentially "repent and believe," yet it must be singularly applied to each seeker. Our conveyor belt approach to conversion results in glib assurances of salvation, but in no sense of servanthood or creaturehood. We approach God as casually as we approach the ordering of a pizza. Since we speak of presidents on a first name basis, why the need for 'respect' for the One who also was man and could speak man's language?

Familiarity has bred contempt, and it shows in our churches. I recall my father's telling me of the Welsh revival at the turn of the century, of his going to chapel every morning, of my grandfather's going down into the coal mines singing the praises of Jehovah. But there was also a deep conviction of sin because the joyous, singing Welsh also had a grasp of the nature and holiness of God. I came to Christ in the quiet of my own room as a teen-ager. I had been impressed by the description of the gambling at the cross in Douglas's book, *The Robe*, and by the fact that Christ had died there for my sin. Do you know what struck me in that hour of conversion? That God was holy, and I was going to hell if I didn't receive Christ as my Savior. There was fear and there were tears because the Holy Spirit had confronted me with the holiness of God and the evil of my sins.

Now people skip into the kingdom with less emotion than taking out a mortgage on a too expensive home. This is not to suggest that apprehending God and worshipping Him should be synonymous with sadness and sobriety, but we could stand a dose of that as contrasted with the flippancy of an age which stands on the doorstep of nuclear holocaust. Must not we who stand in the pulpit bear some of the fault? Are we so busy seeking success that we leave people with a mechanistic, utilitarian view of a God who does for us, rather than of the character of the God who is for us?

The psalmist said, "The fear of the Lord is the beginning of wisdom:" (Ps. 111:10). We do well to consider some of the blessings which result from a holy and healthy fear of God. First, the fear of God brings progress in our walk with God. The psalmist wrote, "Who is the man who fears the Lord? God will instruct him in the way he should choose" (Ps. 25:12). The Scriptures use a variety of words for the English word *fear*. Essentially, these words, when related to believers, do not convey the image of phobic fear, a fear which is negative.

The fear of God is intended to be a wholesome experience in which we see the greatness, the awesomeness of God. The cumulative impact of considering the various attributes of God is to inculcate this soul-piercing awareness of Creator/creature relationship. When the matter of our sin is then considered, it magnifies the sense of apartness from God. But the gap is spanned as we see in Christ the mediator (in Latin, "the bridge") who brings Creator/creature together at Calvary.

Churches need this dimension to experience true worship. We suffer from a concept of grace which allows for a flippant coziness with Deity! David was telling us in Psalm 25 that a sense of direction is in proportion to our fear of God. He then added the corollary in verse 14, "The secret of the Lord is for them that fear him."

As we move on in God's way, this awe of who He is then brings His instruction. Arbitrary appropriation of power and authority is decried in Scripture. The secrets of God are revealed to those who cultivate this intimacy with Him.

Another blessing which comes from fearing God is that of protection. The psalmist warned that armies and weapons of warfare are not man's real hope for national or personal security. This is not to suggest that in this political jungle of our times we dare trust our security to atheistic forces which seek to lull others by treaties. Such treaties are made to be broken, to deceive in order to enslave. How dreamy some Christians have become in these matters.

But our ultimate security is in our reliance on the Lord, or as Psalm 33:18 puts it, "Behold, the eye of the Lord is upon them that fear him." He sees our predicaments and intervenes on our behalf "to deliver from death" and "to keep alive in famine" (Ps. 33:19).

How well I remember the darkness, the rain, the savage force of that tornado in 1969. How appropo are the words of David, "The angel of the

Lord encamps around those who fear Him" (Ps. 34:7, NIV). In a situation in which his life was at stake, David recognized that a holy fear of God gave to him a providential insulation from the fear of man. We desperately need the surrounding protection of God to care for us in the face of "this present pornographic age" as Paul wrote.

What better illustration of divine protection than that of the crisis days of Hezekiah and Isaiah. Sennacherib's forces threatened the very existence of Judah, but the king and the prophet who feared God were filled with righteous anger at the taunting words of the Assyrians, "Will your God save you?" In an incident difficult to grasp, God smote 185,000 Assyrians before the walls of Jerusalem, a dramatic illustration of His ability to aid His own when in dire straits (2 Kings 19).

The fear of God also brings provision. Most believers in this country know little of physical deprivation. Even our poor are rich as compared to the poor of India. Apart from occasional gasoline shortages, this generation has known little deprivation. Their world is one of abundance. How then do we relate to Psalm 34:9, "O fear the Lord, you His saints; for to those who fear Him there is no want" (NASB). Perhaps we need to file this verse away against a future time when food is scarce or when yet unknown forces demand renunciation of our faith for food.

But we have another need for provision, for we do not live by bread alone. We have the capacity of a spiritual appetite. As we need a physical daily bread, so we need a daily portion of spiritual bread. In this context of pointing out God's provision for the physical, David underscored the importance of the spiritual, "They who seek the Lord shall not be in want of any good thing" (Ps. 34:10, NASB).

As we anticipate an uncertain future, we rest in the promise of God's provision. However, we need to immunize ourselves now against future privation by seeking the Lord first, thus accepting the premise that "the other things" will be added to us. We must prepare for days of stress and scarcity. Christians would do well to simplify their life styles and ease away from luxury and self-pampering. Hard times will surely come, and God will provide for us in them, but let us set our course now.

"Come, you children, listen to me; I will teach you the fear of the Lord" (Ps. 34:11, NASB). Our Lord said, "Fear not them which kill the body, but are not able to kill the soul: but rather fear him which is able to destroy both soul and body in hell" (Matt. 10:28). As we seek (fear) the Lord, He meets our needs, even as He keeps our lives in focus. We are citizens of another kingdom, one not of this world.

This indefinable fear/faith we struggle to define begins to reveal itself in a pattern. Progress into the life of faith brings us into situations in which we need His protection and His provision, and such progress begins to unfold His purpose for us. Indeed the fear of God brings the blessing of discovering His *purpose* for life.

We are moving toward the heart of the matter. As already seen, God blesses the God-fearer in all aspects of life, but here is where the Christian comes to a spiritual crossroads. Shall he be occupied with the presents of God, what He gives, or with the presence of God, who He is? It is a fine distinction, to be sure. The Church today seems taken with the presents of God. But the psalmist recorded, "The Lord favors those who fear Him" (Ps. 147:11, NASB).

Wrestle with me over this concept of the fear of God—this blend of trust, awe, God-attraction, self-revulsion, mystery, yet knowledge. It is what one has carefully called "God-intoxication." Is this some isolating mysticism? No, we have to be consciously involved in a real world, but when our inner beings are free from outer pressures, our soul flies to thoughts of the Lord—what Tozer called "the magnetic north of the soul."

Is not that the spirit seen in the first five verses of Psalm 145? Here is human language breathing an atmosphere of sheer praise to the Lord. "Great is the Lord, and greatly to be praised. One generation shall praise thy works to another, and shall declare thy mighty acts" (vv. 3-4). Note that! "THY works and THY mighty acts." Not so-and-so's great church or ministry. Aware that it is God working in us, we see that our purpose is to focus our lives on Him and then, "He will fulfill the desire of those who fear Him" (Ps. 145:19, NASB).

Our ultimate desire must always mesh with

that of the Son of Man in His earthly ministry—to do the will of the Father. That will is discerned through the Word and then discovered in the world. "Blessed is every one that feareth the Lord; that walketh in his ways" (Ps. 128:1). Wonder and work blend together as our souls occupy earth yet rush for our magnetic north, Jesus Christ. Yes, fear of God is life on the highest plane, that necessary backdrop to His love and mercy.

Of unrepentant mankind, Paul had to write, "There is no fear of God before their eyes" (Rom. 3:18). For the Church the need is great for a cleansing which will allow an unquenched and ungrieving Holy Spirit to manifest the presence of God so that there will be a manifestation of both the repulsing and attracting fear of God. Then the results of Acts 5 shall be repeated in our times, "And great fear came upon all the church, and upon as many as heard these things" (Acts 5:11).

May churches step back from the tangent of gifts and presents to the touchstone of Giver and Presence that this generation may also praise and rehearse the mighty acts of God to the next. May we again move in that holy and rarified air of the fear of the Lord, and then shall we accomplish the purpose of God in our corporate and individual worship of Him and service for Him.

10

The Authority of God

I read a statement recently which keeps returning to my thoughts. "Behind every heretical ecclesiology lies an heretical Christology." Look around at some of the mainline churches in your community and ask yourself how they got so far out of touch with the gospel. Their ecclesiastical aberrations are really the terminal signs of a more serious spiritual sickness. Death theologically came earlier when weakened positions on the person and work of Christ were countenanced.

No right thinking evangelical would have problems with the above, but unconsciously the success syndrome has created a new Christological crisis in the church. Busy Christians, taken with the American concept of the gross national product, have rallied to the motto, "Big is Best." The result in the churches is a gross nominal product—mini-saints, saved so as by fire, yet hardly discernable from the worldling, apart from the scorecard.

But to foster the size concept, the local church must put its eggs in the basket of the professionals, especially the father figure who appears on Sunday, and then disappears the rest of the week. The R. Roland Ruhles are in abundance and have assumed an authority in the churches never intended for man. Manuals on church growth make it plain that the authority vested in the local body will have to be passed on to the professional decision-makers at the top.

Historians acknowledge of democracy what may also be true of local autonomy in the church, "That it is the best, and the worst form of government." But there also are checks and balances as well as practical involvements which indicate that there is more wisdom among the laity than some in the clergy want to recognize.

Whereas the liberal becomes too familiar with Christ by glorying in His life, we tend to keep Him at a distance by emphasizing His death. Yet He rose from the grave, and He must rule in a conscious way in the church. If we wonder at the parade of bizarre goings-on today in churches, we find but mere repetition of past problems. As one has well said, "If history teaches us anything, it is that history teaches us nothing."

Paul faced such a potpourri of error in the Colossian situation. Jewish legalism, Greek gnosticism, mixtures of both, and a few other ingredients made for a rather avante-garde fellowship. We detect Paul's concern when he warned: "I say this in order that no one may delude you with persuasive argument. . . . See to it that no one takes you captive through philosophy and empty deception, according to the tradition of men, according to the elementary principles of the world, rather than according to Christ. . . . Therefore let no one act as your judge in regard to food or drink or in respect to a festival or a new moon or a Sabbath day" (Col. 2:4, 8, 16, NASB).

Only the labels change on doctrinal tangents and heresies. The apostle desired to restore spiritual sanity; thus he moved quickly to the attack. His arguments about what was acceptable and where true authority should reside in the church could be summarized in his statement, "He is also head of the body, the Church; and He is the beginning, the first-born from the dead; so that He Himself might come to have first place in everything" (Col. 1:18, NASB).

Current trends indicate the need for a fresh emphasis on this truth: "Christ is the Head of the Church." For when we tamper with that cornerstone, when we abdicate to men authority which belongs to Christ, then our ecclesiology so weakened will inevitably crumble. And we are seeing increased disenchantment with the superpastor mentality as more clerical Achilles-heel weaknesses are coming to light.

As we pursue the theme of the sovereignty of Christ in the Church as seen in Colossians, we need to ask two questions. First, what is the basis for this sovereignty? The Christian has been brought into a relationship with the one on whom many titles have been bestowed. He is our King, "who hath delivered us from the power of darkness, and hath translated us into the kingdom of his dear Son" (Col. 1:13). In an era of emphasis on personal and civil rights, it is most difficult for believers to think of the king/servant relationship. Such does not change the facts. One day He shall reign visibly on this earth; but now, as it were, He is to reign invisibly on this earth through the Church. The very familiar Romans 10:9-10 not only outlines the overt means to salvation, but also endorses the missing message of the lordship of Christ!

The apostle moved back another step to teach that Christ is indeed the eternal one. He did not commence existence at Bethlehem. This seals the reality of redemption. No mere man died as an example on the cross. But the God-Man died there, "who his own self bare our sins in his own body on the tree" (1 Pet. 2:24). This is the great enigma of our faith—unbelievably believable. What? That the one whose environment and work area is eternity "should taste death for every man" (Heb. 2:9). Yet there it is, Christ is, "the image of the invisible God, the firstborn of every creature" (Col. 1:15). Were God, in His ultimate essence, to look into a mirror, He would see Jesus Christ! That is the grand seal of salvation, the eternity of the Redeemer.

A careful brief was being established by Paul in this Colossian letter. Right from the outset he anticipated arguments which would develop through the centuries. And as a happy fringe benefit, he added that Jesus Christ is both creator and sustainer of the universe: "For by him all things were created," and "In Him all things hold together" (Col. 1:16, 17, NIV). Indeed, for one with such authority and power, is submission by and in the Church too unrealistic an expectation?

Then, after this overwhelming recitation of the greatness and glory of Christ, Paul came to his conclusion, a needed antidote for any church enamored with man and the ways of man. "And he is the head of the body, the church: who is the beginning, the first-born from the dead; that in all things he might have the preeminence" (Col. 1:18). Paul was not only using a physical analogy, but also employing the word *head* with its ingrained meaning of authority. Christ is the head of the Church because He is its Creator, a creation rooted in redemption/resurrection; therefore in everything He is to have the preeminence. Lest the point be missed, Paul added this magnificent afterthought, "For it pleased the Father that in him should all fulness dwell" (Col. 1:19).

He is the redeemer who is more than enough. What a shame that in too many churches men act as if they were the fourth person of the Godhead with an arrogance more in tune with Romans 7 than Romans 8. How little of the *doulos* spirit is behind the sacred desk these days! What a void needs to be filled with a new submission to the doctrine and demeanor of Jesus Christ! Why is there such a preoccupation with man and marginal matters when Christ is and offers all that we need? Away with the religious vaudeville! Away with an "evangelical deism" which allows God to save us, but then be dismissed while we launch out in the flesh to do His work.

The Scriptures do not say, "We will build our church," but "I will build my church" (Matt. 16:18). Immediately after describing who Christ is, Paul added further light, "In whom are hid all the treasures of wisdom and knowledge" (Col. 2:3). I recognize the seeming unreality of the thesis, let the Lord control the local church, for it keeps bogging down in committees, moss-backed tradition, and church busyness. But if it is His Church, and He has the wisdom we need to conduct it, then why do we not submit to His leadership?

The final answer to our first question is supremely and sublimely recorded in Colossians 2:9-10, "For in him dwelleth all the fulness of the Godhead bodily. And ye are complete in him, which is the head. . ." Fullness in the Son is the basis for completion in Him personally and collectively. Well, then, will someone explain why all these "saintlets" are running around seeking experiences when in Christ they should have experienced completeness from the seeker of their souls? Why are we reaching for the exotic, when we possess all we need by abiding in the vine? How this generation needs a dose of dogma from John 15!

The second question is, what is the practical outworking of the sovereignty of Christ in the Church? The main portion of Colossians is a pragmatic delineation of the theme. Yet even in the midst of all the admonitions and instruction, the apostle had a grasp of what was basic to the entire issue—the will of God. He had begun the epistle with a statement to that effect, "Paul, an apostle of Jesus Christ by the will of God" (Col. 1:1).

The will of God seems to be an evasive concept for many Christians. They view it as something both mysterious and mystical. It need not be. The objective will of God is essentially the great amalgam of truth in Scripture which calls all believers to account. The subjective will of God is that which specifically involves the individual Christian in the unique task of life to which he has been called by God.

Subjectively, Paul was called to be an apostle—a specially commissioned individual to preach the gospel to the Gentiles. Paul indicated that when each believer is in the will of God, then there is health in the church, and Christ is sovereign in practice. Thus Paul prayed, "We have not ceased to pray for you and to ask that you may be filled with the knowledge of His will" (Col. 1:9, NASB). At the close of the epistle Paul pointed to the mutual concern of Epaphras for the Colossian believers, stating that he was always laboring earnestly for you in his prayers, that you may stand perfect and fully assured in all the will of God" (Col. 4:12, NASB). "In all the will of God"— does not one find here the idea of a strata of life with Christ which is full and fulfilling because of discovering "the all" of God's will? Epaphras, the servant of Christ, labored in prayer that the Colossians would find this fullness.

Imagine a church populated with Christians

eager to discern and experience the will of God! When such occurs, the warning of Colossians 2:19 can be put into the positive, "...holding fast to the head, from whom the entire body, being supplied and held together by the joints and ligaments, grows with a growth which is from God" (NASB). There is the key, "grows with a growth which is from God"—not a growth which has to be conjured up and cajoled along by the energy of man, but a growth "from God." Dare we long for such a divine, life-giving spontaneity of growth!

Let us then, in response to this immediate context, get off tangents, however alluring they may appear. Rather let us fix ourselves in Christ, the Head of the Church, who alone can give lasting increase. If we follow the ways of man, then the product will be strictly human. But if we seek the will of God, then the results will bear the stamp of divine approval.

Only as death works in us (Col. 1:22) can life and maturity work out through us. Did not Paul offer some rudimentary pattern for our churches that we might accomplish God's will in our local churches? Let our standard reside in this basic admonition, "As ye have therefore received Christ Jesus the Lord, so walk ye in him: rooted and built up in him, and stablished in the faith, as ye have been taught, abounding therein with thanksgiving" (Col. 2:6-7).

As we begin with simple faith in Christ, so let us continue in the church, rooted in Him and longing to see His unique will achieved as glory accrues not to men, but to the Son of Man, Jesus Christ.

III.   Serving

11

First Things First

The very nature of the days in which we live demands that the church establish priorities. We cannot do everything, but we can do something. We cannot be everywhere, but we can be somewhere. The flock of God cowers in the pews assailed by demands on their time and money, as each visiting expert adds to the burden with yet another seminar or sector of service to be considered. Thus many Christians are perpetually in spring training, constantly preparing, though seldom in the lineup.

Our churches have also become bedlams of activity, yet the quality of the product seems to diminish in proportion to the increased busyness. The latest rage is to lay on people a guilt complex for failure to involve themselves in social issues. It may sound archaic and out of step, but the church's mission is ever redemptive. Does it seem too calloused to say that our good deeds should always have the ultimate goal of bringing individuals to Christ?

Our Lord insisted, "The Son of man is come to seek and to save that which was lost" (Luke 19:10). His teaching and miracles were a part of the divine magnet to draw the lost to Himself. But the devil, the master deceiver, has blazed all kinds of tangential trails for believers to tread. Is it too simplistic to offer a basic pattern by which to evaluate what we are doing?

Four key areas appear to stand out in the New Testament. They are 1) *Koinonia*, fellowship with God and His people; 2) *Didache*, teaching and instruction in the Word of God; 3) *Kerygma*, proclamation of the gospel; and 4)*Diakonia*, ministry to people in the name of Christ.

How we need to evaluate against such crucial concepts the proliferation of groups and activities in the church! Let us consider each of these precepts. First, there is *koinonia*. The root of fellowship is in a personal relationship to God through Christ. John dealt with this in the initial chapter of his first epistle. Verses 1 and 2 describe the importance of personal knowledge and contact with Jesus Christ, with the realization that this unique life was God manifest in the flesh. But the price of such a relationship is centered in the grace of God, and that couched in sacrifice, "And the blood of Jesus Christ his Son cleanseth us from all sin" (1 John 1:7b). The commencement and continuation of this blessed friendship with God always confronts the tragic existence of sin and the constant need for cleansing and forgiveness. Despite the special acquaintanceship with the Son, John was so awed by this relationship that he later wrote, "Behold, what manner of love the Father hath bestowed upon us, that we should be called the sons of God. . ." (1 John 3:1). Are you a name-dropper? I have known a few celebrities, and I must confess to enjoying people's reaction to my having known some famous person. But what is that compared to having a personal tie to the living God! Little wonder that John exclaimed as he did about such knowledge.

This fellowship with God produces a Christ-centered fellowship with other believers. *Koinonia* signifies "a sharing in common" and "a basis of friendship." Thus John pointed out that having "seen and heard," the Christian then declares this truth to others in order that "Ye also may have fellowship with us: and truly our fellowship [*koinonia*] is with the Father, and with his Son Jesus Christ" (1 John 1:3). Clearly the object was to focus on Christ—not on plans, programs, or an exalting of people.

This kind of sharing, as compared to what passes for sharing in modern times, reveals a great chasm between the two. Current sharing too often inflates Adam at the expense of the Second Adam, but the sharing of the apostles was rooted in deep spiritual issues. It involved honesty and walking in the light, with an awareness of personal sin so that the blood of Jesus Christ could cleanse from all sin (1 John 1:7).

Such is a far cry from the rampant worship of the Drs. Ruhles of our times and a new Protestantism which holds to the infallibility of the preacher. The godly man will not need such props, for his heart is fixed on God, and he will quickly admit his fallibility by submitting to the truths of 1 John 1:8-9. This entire context breathes of a refreshing obedience to God and of a discreet openness with the brethren, something which is sadly lacking today. Such fellowship will banish trivialities and will knit pastor and people in a spiritual wedlock which places one's relationship to God as the key issue, for from this will flow, or not flow, spiritual vitality.

A second area to consider as a priority for the Church is *didache*, teaching and instruction in the Word of God. Is it unkind to say that our churches are filled with biblical illiterates? Little wonder when so much of Christian literature today is a gimmicky potpourri of "how to's" and "how do you feel" or "what do you think?" It is not pious platitude to urge a return to "thus saith the Lord."

That amazing Old Testament character Moses, who had an experience with God which would have kept him in demand in every Bible conference in our land, still prioritized the communication of divine revelation over "felt needs." He commanded the priests, "Gather the people together, men, and women, and children, and thy stranger who is within thy gates, that they may *hear*, and that they may *learn*, and fear the Lord your God, and observe to do all the words of this law" (Deut. 31:12).

What tales he could have spun about his experience with God, of seeing the back parts of God and surviving, yet in his farewell address to Israel, he emphasized not experience, but the written expression of God's will, His Word. The lesson was not lost on his understudy, Joshua. As he prepared to lead the people across the Jordan into the land Moses could not enter, Joshua sounded a call to courage and then a significant reminder, "This book of the law shall not depart out of thy mouth; but thou shalt meditate therein day and night, that thou mayest observe to do according to all that is written therein: for then thou shalt make thy way prosperous, and then thou shalt have good success" (Josh. 1:8).

These pioneers of the faith were doers, not dreamers; however, they understood the importance of the ingestion and then implementation of the Word of God. If your heart is as dull and slow as mine, you need the consistent probing and provision afforded by systematic feeding on and instruction from the Scriptures. The greatest apologetic for the gospel remains a transformed life, and that directs us to the purpose for the Scriptures.

The great touchstone of truth for the purpose of Scripture is, of course, Paul's word to Timothy. In passing it is important to note that in the pastoral epistles Paul admonished the leaders of the churches to put at the top of their list, the teaching and preaching of the Word. A literal translation of the beginning of 2 Timothy 3:16 is, "All Scripture is God-breathed." With what beauty and dynamic that economy of words speaks of the origin and the operation of Holy Writ. In the autographs, as a reflection of the very nature of God, the Scriptures were inerrant. Why is that so difficult to accept? God looked on this special written creation and said, "It is very good." Would He commence with imperfection what He chose to use for perfection?

The purpose of Scripture? Salvation! Thus Paul warned Timothy about false teachers, even as he reminded him of that holy nucleus in his family who applied to his life the ". . .scriptures, which are able to make thee wise unto salvation through faith which is in Christ Jesus" (2 Tim. 3:15). Let us not draw back from constant and continual use of the Scriptures. Humanism has but stoked a near explosive volcano of events which it cannot control, but the Word of God is both lamp and light in a modern maze of distraction and despair.

Only the powerful Word can deal with the issue of the inherent inhumanity of man outside of Christ, and likewise Paul went on to describe the goal of redemption as centered first on who He is, and then on what He does. Our generation has switched the order, and we suffer badly because of it. 2 Timothy 3:16-17 makes it plain that what a man becomes is very much predicated on what he thinks. The application of sound doctrine results in the smoothing of rough edges and what, accompanied by positive principles in right living, results in mature individuals in Christ. These god-like ones then have the capacity to produce a variety of good works. The Puritans, ever concerned about the root of the matter, would be quizzical at our attempts to produce good works apart from spiritual maturity. To reverse the order is to introduce spiritual strangulation. Dr. Tozer well pinpointed the issue, "Preoccupation with appearances and a corresponding neglect of the out-of-sight root of the true spiritual life are prophetic signs which go unheeded. Religious pragmatism is running wild among the orthodox. There is but one test for the religious leaders; success. Everything is forgiven him except failure."[1]

As Paul had diagramed the order for the transmission of truth (2 Tim. 2:2), he also underlined the import of the place of faithful and reliable men, proven entities in the divine enterprise. Thus in the passage in 2 Timothy 3, we see Paul clothing the godly servant in the garb of the Word. Dare we do less in our various ministries in the church?

The third priority for the Church follows very closely to fellowship and teaching. It is the *kerygma*, the declaration of the message of redemption to the lost. I recall witnessing to a fellow draftee in the army, a graduate of MIT. He stumbled over the idea of lostness as I sought to define it for him. Still it is a word too important to replace, for it pictures someone wandering around, uncertain of his direction. The lost need to stop and get directions.

In essence evangelism entails telling the lost that they are operating out of a past of sin and sins, that they are heading for a disastrous future while presently frustrated in seeking meaning to life. The Book of Acts is filled with sermons of a kerygmatic nature, dealing with past and future while calling individuals to an accounting with God in the present.

The simplest form of the *kerygma* is found in 1 Corinthians 15:3-5a in the expression of the verbs *died, buried, rose,* and *seen.* That is the framework of the gospel proclamation. Other New Testament sermons reveal data conveyed about the life and ministry of Christ, followed by an insistence on personal response to the message in terms of repentance and faith, with the underlying warning of a future judgment. Obviously, to speak of his death necessitated a consideration of His life and Who He was! Belief in the resurrection was pivotal, especially as seen in Romans 10:9-10, for it also presupposed the reception of the doctrine of the deity of Christ.

There is an interlocking aspect about Scripture which comes to the fore in the basic truths related to salvation. Truth builds upon truth, but with what result? Paul described it in Ephesians 1:13, "In whom ye also trusted, after that ye heard the word of truth, the gospel of your salvation: in whom also after that ye believed, ye were sealed with that holy Spirit of promise."

Scripture reveals the continuous activity of the Holy Spirit. He breathed into dust, and man became a living soul. But sin caused Him, in some sense, to flee His residence in man after the fall. Then He breathed afresh into men to give that inerrant Word man needed to see his need. And the

Spirit now breathes through Scripture to fan conviction and produce that holy spark of life which leads to faith. Then, as before the fall, the Spirit is able to reside in vessels of flesh, as so visibly demonstrated on the day of Pentecost.

Hearing, trusting, sealing—these terms describe the pilgrimage to new life in Christ. The servant in Ephesus identified his master's logs from upstream forests by the seal or mark on those logs adrift in the Cayster River as it flowed past that city. Likewise the Christian is identified by the sealing presence of the Holy Spirit, which sealing bespeaks ownership and security. It is a very fine line between sealing and seeming legalism, yet we must insist on a verification of real life. "The Spirit itself beareth witness with our spirit, that we are children [the born ones] of God" (Rom. 8:16). Therefore, since He is the Spirit who is holy, there should also be a change in the life style of the one who trusts in Christ. The awesome words of Matthew 7 about professed believers warn us that mouthing orthodox words does not always indicate being mastered by the Word. "By their fruits ye shall know them" (Matt. 7:20).

Out of the above, there arises a concern for the spiritual welfare of others. No foothold for pride is to be found in that mountain of grace where all are guests by divine invitation. There is so very much being written these days about church growth, and much of it valuable. But there is the danger of being lulled into thinking that there is some sure-fire formula which, when followed, will cause automatic church explosion.

The Book of Acts records that following the death of Stephen, "They that were scattered abroad went everywhere preaching the word" (Acts 8:4). Is not the primary way of evangelism what the visionary Roland Allen reaffirmed during his years as a missionary in China (1895-1903)? He spoke of spontaneous expansion or the indigenous concept when he wrote of, "That expansion which follows the unexhorted and unorganized activity of individual members of the Church explaining to others the Gospel which they have found for themselves."[2]

Why must our churches be so seminared and organized to do what is an individual responsibility? Why must we make complicated what God has made simple?

Each of us returning to our mini-worlds has the privilege and the responsibility to reach people we know. This surely does not rule out other methods of evangelism, yet here is where we are hurting. The trail keeps winding back to that first point, *koinonia*, our relationship to the Lord and the reality of His life in ours. Without that, we are chanting clichés or trying to add bodies to buildings. Rather Paul zeroed in on the crux of the matter, "I am debtor both to the Greeks, and to the Barbarians; both to the wise, and to the unwise" (Rom. 1:14). Christians in this land are too acquainted with the concept of debt. Our nation struggles under a massive national debt while individuals live on a "possess now, pay later" approach to finances. But the debt of which Paul writes is a spiritual obligation to pass on the gospel to people of every segment of society. Salvation is not universal, but particular in its application. The best method is one to one. Mass evangelism via the media surely should be used, but personal confrontation is the most telling way to share the gospel.

But we must beware of viewing evangelism as a drudgery and a burdensome necessity. The apostle could also say in the same breath as the above, "I am not ashamed of the gospel of Christ: for it is the power of God unto salvation to every one that believeth; to the Jew first, and also to the Greek" (Rom. 1:16). He knew the transforming effectiveness of that message in his life, and he was utterly persuaded as to the veracity and authenticity of his relationship to Christ. Therefore, he would not hesitate to share that message, for he personally knew its power.

In retrospect, one begins to see that these key areas of priority for the church build upon one another. True fellowship with the Lord radiates out to the brethren and creates an environment for longing to know the Word of God. Then there results a fully orbed teaching of the Word, with a holding to the main issues. Fellowship with such teaching produces mature believers who make a commitment to proclaim the message of redemption. We cannot leave *kerygma* to a handful of media personalities. Real church growth will result as individuals penetrate their worlds, not only with the message, but with the crucial method, the reality of Christ in their lives!

The fourth area of priority for the Church centers in *diakonia* or ministry. Obviously there is a correlation between preaching the gospel and a concern for people's physical needs. I preached my first sermon in the mission founded by the beloved Fanny Crosby in Bridgeport, Connecticut. It was in a rundown part of town, and indigent men had to attend chapel service to ensure receipt of a meal and a place to sleep. Without going into the sad details, the shift in emphasis in that mission went from the spiritual to the physical until finally services were dropped as more commercial matters gained control.

That danger always exists. We have to focus on the soul which lasts forever over the body which exists merely for time. Evangelicals need not be shamed by a supposed lack of concern for the total man. Our missionary endeavors do minister to the total man far more than those ideological snipers who say we simply offer "pie in the sky" to a needy world. But the redemptive must take priority, and the Scriptures remind us that charity begins at home when it comes to the matter of ministry.

The well-known passage in Acts 6 describes the early Church's handling of a practical need. The apostles made it plain that physical provision for man must never interfere with the spiritual well-being of man, "It is not desirable for us to neglect the word of God in order to serve tables" (Acts 6:2). In no sense was this a demeaning attitude toward physical need in the establishment of priorities. The apostles were wise enough to see that a practical solution was needful lest a division be caused in the fellowship, but they could not afford to be sidetracked from committing themselves "to prayer and the ministry of the word" (Acts 6:4).

In the Coverdale translation of 1535, this passage quaintly speaks of "the daily hand-reaching." Such graphic description reminds us of the millions reaching out for physical nourishment. We must do what we can to sustain physical life in people in order to prolong their opportunity to receive spiritual life. If Christians gave one dollar for every pound they are overweight, we could reach countless multitudes of people.

Paul wrote, "And whatsoever ye do in word or deed, do all in the name of the Lord Jesus. . ." (Col. 3:17). The good works must always be coupled with the good Word. To minister in His name is to share the meaning of that name. He is our best example: "For even the Son of man did not come to be served, but to serve [minister], and to give his life a ransom for many" (Mark 10:45). Let us not be stampeded into a guilt trip because we want to honor the priorities of Scripture.

I recall walking in a downtown area a few years ago on a cold, wintry day. I had read Matthew 25 that morning in the study. Up ahead I could see a bedraggled looking man working his way through the crowd, asking for money. I started to edge away toward the curb hoping to avoid him when the words, "I was hungry, and you gave me something to eat," stabbed my conscience. I turned around, stopped the individual, bought a warm meal for him, and shared the gospel as well. That was hardly a sacrificial act on my part, but it points up the importance of combining spiritual and physical ministry.

Have we professionals penned up the sheep in a stockade of seeming spiritual inferiority? Do we dampen their first love by insisting on formats or formulae by which they can minister, not trusting them to allow the Spirit to guide them into fields of usefulness? They need to be delivered from the bondage to degrees and special training. Well worth repeating are the oft-quoted words of Vance Havner: "Never before in the history of the Church have we had so many degrees, and yet so little temperature!" The unschooled and undegreed Peter and John bespoke a vitality in the early Church which all of our academic excellence has not repeated in the Church today.

The Church needs to return to the basics by a reaffirmation of its priorities. Fellowship, teaching the Word, proclamation, and ministry are the building blocks of real church growth. Blessed by the Lord of the Church, Jesus Christ, these elements will produce a growth in the Church both real in quality and realistic in quantity!

1. Tozer, *The Best of A. W. Tozer*, p. 118.
2. Roland Allen, *The Spontaneous Expansion of the Church* (Grand Rapids: Wm. B. Eerdmans Publishing Company, 1962), p. 7.

12

Right Person—Right Place—Right Time

The Book of Acts can best be approached in terms of a series of threes. First, three arrows: one going up to remind us of the Ascension; one coming down to remind us of the day of Pentecost; and one going out to remind us of the persecution of the Church which sent believers out preaching the gospel. Then, three cities: Jerusalem, where the gospel came to the Jew; Antioch of Syria, where the gospel blended with Jew and Gentile; and Rome, where the gospel took hold among Gentiles. Finally, three divisions: Acts 1-7, outreach to the Jew; Acts 8-12, outreach to peripheral people associated with Judaism; and Acts 13-28, outreach to the Gentile world.

Thus we observe theological, geographical, and sociological progression in the advancement of the good news of redemption. Acts 8 is a pivotal chapter in the book. In that chapter we observe the example and importance of one man's contacting another for Christ. We need to see in the experience of Philip, the evangelist, those factors which made possible his being used by God to reach a key individual.

Philip was the right person because he first

had been made righteous via repentance and faith. Was Philip present on the day of Pentecost when Peter preached with the newly given power of the Holy Spirit? We are not sure. At any rate he is found in early association with that pioneer group of believers. Philip would prove to be the right person because he was already being used by the Lord. In the incident involving the establishment of the office of deacon, Philip was one of those selected to serve in order that the apostles could concentrate on their major task.

There is a certain apprenticeship Christians must face in serving the Lord. God does not entrust power and responsibility to the novice; rather, there are levels of opportunity by which an individual's reliability is proven. Philip established this by his ministry in the pragmatic matter of serving tables. He did not feel this was beneath his dignity. He could appreciate the wisdom of using a Greek-speaking Jew to care for the needs of the widows of Hellenistic background. Philip's willingness to serve in this capacity led to an opportunity for a special ministry.

Little did the apostles realize how the mandate of Acts 1:8 would be accomplished. Reverse the numbers, and Acts 8:1 reveals that persecution, spawned by the martyrdom of Stephen, scattered the believers from the environs of Jerusalem. This cameo of truth was recorded by Luke, "Therefore they that were scattered abroad went every where preaching the word" (Acts 8:4). Philip was among these expropriated evangelists,

"Then Philip went down to the city of Samaria, and preached Christ unto them" (Acts 8:5). It is interesting to observe the use of a semi-outsider, a Hellenist, to reach other outsiders.

We today cannot quite fathom the meaning of this step. The simple statement in John 4:9, "the Jews have no dealings with the Samaritans," cloaks a history of agitation and antipathy between the two. Samaritans were looked upon as half-breeds, the by-products of a since past program of Assyrian policies after the defeat of the Northern Kingdom. To the Jews, Samaritans were racial and religious outcasts. Although a Jew himself, though not of Jerusalem, Philip perhaps detected something of an aloofness in those natives of Zion, at least before the day of Pentecost.

But Philip was open and flexible enough to recognize the value of a soul regardless of any personal prejudices. God so blessed His servant that, "there was much rejoicing in that city [Samaria]" (Acts 8:8, NASB). Pause to note the progression. Great persecution (Acts 8:1) produced great sorrow (Acts 8:2) which led to great joy (Acts 8:8). The tears of the saints still need to water the planting of the gospel.

Philip was also the right man because he was obedient. In the midst of a tremendous outpouring of the blessing of God, he was ordered to leave Samaria. What might he have said? "Lord, I'm in the midst of a revival. I'm supposed to be interviewed on KSAM tonight. They want me to found a school in this town." Despite the apparent absurdity of leaving such scenes of blessing to go to a desert place, Philip still obeyed the Lord (Acts 8:26-27). This man of God displayed a sweet spirit which needs to be followed today. He was willing to wait on tables and willing to leave the limelight simply on the say-so of God.

He was the right man in the right place. He left the success of Samaria for the sands of Gaza. He had an appointment with a man who could eventually influence many lives. What would be the mathematical probability of two individuals meeting under such circumstances? It would be infinitesimally small. Yet, by divine appointment they met. The Ethiopian eunuch had achieved a measure of success in life, but sensed the deeper needs of his soul. "He had come to Jerusalem to worship" (Acts 8:27b, NASB). A Gentile God-fearer, an outsider in terms of geography, he would most likely have been held at arm's length by right-thinking Jews because he was a eunuch (Deut. 23:1).

Having completed his pilgrimage, the Ethiopian now headed for home (Acts 8:28). His primary purpose had been to worship, but he may have experienced only sharper pangs of spiritual desire, for he left Jerusalem without that inner satisfaction he had been seeking. Doubtless a man of his rank would have traveled in a sizable caravan with a large number of vehicles. Thus the significance of the words, "And the Spirit said to Philip, 'Go up and join this chariot'" (Acts 8:29, NASB). It had to be *this chariot* because it contained the man who had been prepared for Philip. Paul's words are appropriate here, "For all who are being led by the Spirit of God, these are the sons of God" (Rom. 8:14). Both in internal piety as well as external practice, the leading of the Spirit is the ultimate proof of the new birth experience.

Philip was the right man in the right place at the right time. The chronology of this meeting reveals not coincidence, but providence. If this were by mere chance, any number of trivial factors involving just minutes could have kept the two from their appointment. As there was preparation in terms of time, so there was preparation in terms of temperament. Philip was a flexible servant in the hand of God. He could identify with an outsider, be he Samaritan or Ethiopian.

Was part of the eunuch's identification by Philip revealed in the then custom of reading aloud, hence Philip recognized the passage in question from the Suffering Servant section of Isaiah? The evangelist went right to the heart of the issue, "Do you understand what you are reading?" (Acts 8:30, NASB). He didn't ask him about his hangups or the frustrations of his prenatal life. He recognized that here was a man shouting spiritually, "I need help!"

Philip did not play games with the man's mind or emotions; he kept his focus on the Scriptures and the Savior. There followed that classic example for all ministry, and especially for those who preach the Word, "And Philip opened his mouth, and beginning from this Scripture he preached Jesus to him," (Acts 8:35). No matter at what point in Scripture we begin, we must always head for Jesus and the cross. What beautiful timing for Philip to be brought to a seeker at the precise moment he was reflecting on the gospel according to Isaiah, chapter 53!

As is true in most scriptural accounts of events, we do not have all of the conversation and narrative, but we can assume that Philip was persuaded of the genuineness of the eunuch's conversion. Coming from his Gentile background, the Ethiopian, as a proselyte of the gate, had long recognized the importance of baptism. Now his concern was not for identification with Judaism, but for identification with Jesus. We detect that heart-longing in the words, "Look! Water! What prevents me from being baptized?" (Acts 8:36, NASB). No longer was it a question of being on the outer fringe, but rather of the eunuch's now having unhindered fellowship with God and His people. Though verse 37 is deleted in many versions because of textual problems, we can be sure that Philip was satisfied with the Ethiopian's spiritual state. Thus he went with Philip into the waters of baptism and made a public confession of his faith in Christ.

And Philip baptized him. As has been suggested, the man would not have travelled such distances alone and unprotected. What an impact this open stand must have had upon those present in his retinue! Irenaeus later recorded that the Ethiopian became a missionary among his own people. The Ethiopian's conversion was another significant step in the gradual outreach of the gospel from Jew to Gentile along a path of people who had some link with Judaism. God graciously showed the early Church, so close to its Judaistic background, that indeed the prophet Hosea was right when he wrote, "I will say to them which were not my people, 'Thou art my people'" (Hos. 2:23).

But what happened to Philip? Just when the reporters and TV cameras were to record this important ministry and before he could be acclaimed by men, "The Spirit of the Lord snatched Philip away" (Acts 8:39, NASB). How the Church needs men of such a spirit as Philip who are eager only for the glory of God! The Spirit gives us a contrasting example in 3 John where the distinction is made between "Diotrephes, who loveth to have the preeminence" (v. 9) and Demetrius, who "hath good report of all men" (v. 12).

Philip, servant of God that he was, surely realized that one leads those to Christ who have already been led by God and then leaves them with God. Having met God's timetable for the Ethiopian, Philip continued to minister along the coastal road which led him to the north and to Caesarea. There is a postscript to this account of Philip. Twenty years later he was in Caesarea, still serving the Lord, with four daughters who also bore evidence of having been reared by a godly father (Acts 21:8-9). So there was a lasting quality to this man's ministry.

The above can and still happens. I knew of an individual who related his experience on a plane flight to the southwest. He wanted to reach some-one for Christ on that plane and was reading one of Paul Little's books when a conversation began with the man seated next to him. It turned out that both of them had mutual interests and experience in the aircraft industry, in fast-pitch softball, and in the military. The man indicated dissatisfaction with his religious background and was given Little's book, *Know What You Believe* when they reached Phoenix. There was no dramatic conver-sion experience, but there was a modern-day repetition of being the right person in the right place at the right time. When we are what God wants us to be, then we shall be where He wants us to be to do what He wants done.

Does this require the heavy programming seen in churches today? Should not witnessing be as breathing to the Christian? Can we not just be ourselves in the hand of God with a holy relaxation in seeking the lost? Philip's experience reveals the importance of reaching just one person, of being ourselves, and of letting the Spirit move us about as He pleases. But we can be used only as we are obedient and usable.

Real church growth will occur as individual believers are revitalized and bring into the corpor-ate fellowship a holy spontaneity in worship and witness. May God enable us to be as Philip who was the right person in the right place at the right time!

13

The Blessing of Burden

The Scriptures and church history abound with examples of individuals who assumed a burden from God which led to the blessing of God. Such a man was Nehemiah. His life story is that of a man who bore a burden for the work and the honor of God. We need some historical signposts to place Nehemiah. In 537 B.C. the first Jews returned to Jerusalem from Babylon as God fulfilled that marvelous prophecy given to Isaiah concerning the Persian ruler Cyrus. Around 516 B.C. the restoration of the temple was completed. In 479 B.C. Esther became queen of Persia. Then about 458 B.C. Ezra led a second expedition from Babylon. Nehemiah entered the picture as he went to Jerusalem in 445 B.C.

Some 100 years after the first expedition of Jews had entered Jerusalem, they still had not rebuilt the damaged walls about the city. Removed as we are from ancient warfare, we do not grasp the significance of this failure. Walls at that time would be the equivalent of a nuclear deterrent in ours. Without walls, a city was ever at the mercy of warlike predators who roamed the land and of unfriendly neighbors. To resist the enemy and encourage the people, the walls had to be rebuilt.

Moving ahead to the successful conclusion of this task, we see the results, "And at the dedication of the wall of Jerusalem they sought the Levites out of all their places, to bring them to Jerusalem, to keep the dedication with gladness. . ." (Neh. 12:27a). And "that day they offered great sacrifices, and rejoiced: for God had made them rejoice with great joy: the wives also and the children rejoiced: so that the joy of Jerusalem was heard even afar off" (Neh. 12:43).

A deep sense of relief came upon the populace of Jerusalem, for the walls meant security, and they also represented victory over apathy. But this victory was very much the result of, under God, one man with a burden. That man was Nehemiah, who held an important position in the Persian government for, he was the king's cupbearer (Neh. 1:11). This reminds us of Joseph, Moses, and Daniel—believers who attained high office even as they stood for the truths of God. The ancient tyrants they served were often capricious and cruel. One's very life could hang in the balance of their autocratic whims.

One day certain Jews returned to Persia and told Nehemiah that they suffered in the land, ". . .great affliction and reproach: the wall of Jerusalem also is broken down, and the gates thereof are burned with fire" (Neh. 1:3). Sometimes we casually pray about events over which we sense we have no power or control. Nehemiah's prayer breathed the spirit of a man who was burdened for the honor of God. The wonderful deliverance through Cyrus had turned sour because of those unbuilt walls. But Nehemiah, ". . .sat down and wept, and mourned certain days, and fasted, and prayed before the God of heaven" (Neh. 1:4). He then addressed God, not in the flippant, casual way but as ". . .O Lord God of heaven, the great and terrible God. . ." (Neh. 1:5a).

Read the prayer which follows. First Nehemiah confessed his, and then the people's sins. Next he turned to God's Word and the promise of restoration when there was true repentance. Out of that anguish for the honor of God, a plan was born, "Prosper, I pray thee, thy servant this day, and grant him mercy in the sight of this man" (Neh. 1:11). Nehemiah was going to approach the despot in the name of the Lord. Surely the Persian civil service lists bulged with candidates for the position of cupbearer, desirable though dangerous as it was. Nehemiah risked everything. His burden was greater than any concern for personal safety.

God opened the door for Nehemiah to make his request of the king. One day while Nehemiah served the king, the Persian ruler observed that his normally cheerful cupbearer was unhappy. Oh the touch of the human when Nehemiah recorded, "Then I was very sore afraid" (Neh. 2:2). When asked the reason for his sadness, Nehemiah explained the tragic state of affairs in Jerusalem, after which Artaxerxes asked what he could do.

What an insightful statement follows, "So I prayed to the God of heaven" (Neh. 2:4). God wonderfully answered that prayer. Permission was granted for Nehemiah to go to Jerusalem. He was also given authority to claim the resources of the king in rebuilding the wall.

In a way the events which followed were almost anticlimactic. The root of all which took place following Nehemiah's return to Jerusalem was the burden he assumed on hearing of the need. Does this not give us a clue to the present? If the Drs. Ruhles, certainly competent and sincere, are always making the decisions in a local church, at what point do the potential Nehemiahs take on a burden for some part of the work of the Lord? Must we ever defer to professional expertise at the expense of using members of the local body of believers? How will they exercise their gift/gifts of the Spirit if they are quenched by a suffocating layer of professionalism?

Why do we think we can arbitrarily fit people into humanly devised programs? Is it not more reasonable and revelational to see gifts being used by people who catch a vision for some segment of the work because they have a God-given burden for it? As a pastor I must admit that my batting average is far from .1000 in all the decisions I have made in the ministry. If, as some of the experts admit, we must sacrifice congregational involvement in the authority of the local church as the price of size, then we must also accept the consequences of losing the authenticity of a church where God can raise up Nehemiahs to bear burdens, to become blessings. That is too high a price to pay! For when it is said and done, the laymen are the ones at the cutting edge of the church as they mingle in the world on a daily basis. The experts and the Ruhleses are too sequestered in a religious jet set and, far too often, out of touch with the reality of the workaday world. Let us create a climate for Nehemiahs in the Church!

See what can happen! When the Nehemiahs bear God's burdens and exercise their gifts to meet needs, others are mobilized as their abilities are put to work in a constructive manner. That was literally so for those in Jerusalem. The work was divided in order that each would have his part, and each one then recognized how vital it was to accomplish his task. Nehemiah, chapter 3, reveals that wise division of labor. The foreman could walk around the walls of Jerusalem and know at a glance who was working, and who was not.

This transpired because of the concern and the vision of a burden-bearer. Nehemiah had come quietly to Jerusalem, and three days after his arrival, he took a nocturnal stroll about the city to assess the situation. With no fanfare or bravado, he soon had the picture in his mind as he came to the rulers of the city and said, "Come, and let us build up the wall of Jerusalem, that we be no more a reproach" (Neh. 2:17). As he related the events back in Persia which had brought him to their beleaguered city, they responded, "Let us rise up and build" (Neh. 2:18). Clearly, from the context which follows, Nehemiah also had conceived a plan of operation, hence the activity of chapter 3.

The Scriptures make plain the place of leadership, yet the pattern indicates guidance under God rather than under some form of clerical despotism. Nehemiah combined a rare blend of earthly sagacity with heavenly submission. Opposition arose from Sanballat, but Nehemiah countered this in a sensible way, "We made our prayer unto our God, and set a watch against them day and night" (Neh. 4:9). Since the people now had a mind to work, Nehemiah encouraged them to continue to work, though keeping their weapons near at hand (Neh. 4:13, 18).

In the life of a church there are tasks which are long standing. The constant exodus from churches because of population mobility indicates that programming is not enough. There must be a committed segment of burdened people to sustain the growth process; especially is this true in suburbia.

As previously noted, the completion of the wall produced great joy in the city. But Nehemiah's impact did not end there. He was a sensitive man in the hand of God. He repudiated the greed of certain leaders in the city, even as he repulsed the continued efforts of enemies to halt the building effort. He wisely kept in touch with the pulse of the people while seeking to achieve the purposes of God. And he laid the kind of groundwork which furthered the teaching ministry of Ezra.

Nehemiah, the burdened servant of God, was used to bring people into confrontation with their wills and the will of God. The issue focused on the rebuilding of the wall. One is reminded of a similar situation with the prophet Haggai who pointed out that while the people were living "in their wall-to-wall carpeted ranch homes," the house of God stood incomplete.

Nehemiah's commitment led to a restatement of the people's commitment to their God (Neh. 9:36). This was followed by a separation from the world (Neh. 10:28-29), and then there ensued a commitment to the security and welfare of the city of Jerusalem. Do you catch the flow of this? How the people of God are harnessed for the work of God when a man of God puts the honor of God first! Here is not self-seeking, but a burden for the glory of the Lord. Nehemiah's name meant "Jehovah comforts," and God does comfort His people through His servants whom He discomfits to accomplish His will.

The Church will learn only in glory of the eternal value of the life of David Brainerd. Forced to discontinue his theological studies at Yale because of rather critical statements made about the spiritual condition of some of his mentors, David Brainerd soon turned his energies to missionary service among the benighted Indians in the wilderness areas of Pennsylvania and New Jersey. The saga of his devoted service to the Lord and the Indians in those pre-Revolutionary days is the classic illustration, outside of Scripture, of a man with a burden and a vision for the work and glory of God. Who could not be touched by reading the diary of Brainerd as he literally coughed away his brief life seeking to reach those wilderness inhabitants? Although not a success story by modern standards, David Brainerd's life has kindled many another life into service for the King.

How the Church needs a rebirth of a commitment of the caliber of the Nehemiahs and Brainerds! What a significance Nehemiah's ministry had! The walls were rebuilt, the people purified, and the Lord glorified, all because an informed man became burdened and then took steps of action to accomplish the purposes of God.

We have enough experts with their cool professionalism and their automated answers. We need more non-professionals in the local churches who will see needs and then be willing to follow Nehemiah's example, "And it came to pass, when I heard these words, that I sat down and wept, and mourned certain days, and fasted, and prayed before the God of heaven" (Neh. 1:4). How we express our burden-bearing overtly is not the issue, but rather that we ask God to enable us to assume a burden for His honor. Then we shall both begin and persist in the task the Lord reveals to be ours.

What walls need to be rebuilt in the church of which you are a part? There is so very much which needs to be done. The strength of the local church is ever in proportion to that of its members.

14

The Primary Task

"Let us hear the conclusion of the whole matter: Fear God, and keep His commandments: for this is the whole duty of man. For God shall bring every work into judgment, with every secret thing, whether it be good, or whether it be evil" (Eccles. 12:13-14). So spoke the preacher after his searching analysis of life. What is the conclusion of the matter for us centuries later? In this closing section we have considered some bedrock priorities for the Church. What is our mandate for these closing days of human civilization?

Let us put the well-known in a different set of verbal garments. Our primary task is to pass on the presence of God. Would our God, sitting in the heavens, laugh at such an audacious remark? Is He not omnipresent regardless of our efforts? Does not every human bear markings of the image of God anyway? True, but in fulfilling the Great Commission, we are passing on the presence of God in a unique sense.

As individuals respond to the convicting work of the Holy Spirit, they become temples of the Holy Spirit, and the Lord's personalized presence again finds a home in human hearts. This cannot happen apart from genuine repentance and faith, for the Holy Spirit can reside only where the precious blood of the Lamb has brought cleansing from sin. Thus to preach the gospel and see real biblical conversion is to fulfill the primary task of passing on the presence of God. And that is a great contribution—our making sure that the indwelling presence of God is passed on to succeeding generations.

Dr. A. W. Tozer made a distinction between the presence of God and the manifestation of the presence of God. God is present in the believer even when there are times when we are not consciously aware of His presence. He is manifest as we are volitionally aware of His presence. "On our part there must be surrender to the Spirit of God. . .If we cooperate with Him in loving obedience God will manifest Himself to us, and that manifestation will be the difference between a nominal Christian life and a life radiant with the light of His face."[1]

Tozer was not advocating a vain quest after experiences with God, but rather a quest for God Himself. Spiritual shortcuts to power from God do not work. To overcome victoriously in church situations, both pastors and laymen must constantly know the working reality of the presence of God. It is too easy today to be disenchanted by the exhibition of warmed-over carnality cavorting in local fellowships. We need, not something, but Someone, to maintain spiritual balance in the presence of religious imbalance.

But how can we pass on that which we have

not claimed for ourselves? The heart-cry of the Church needs to be, "Lord, go with us!" and "Lord, show us your glory!" These sentences carry us back to the life of Moses. That great statesman of the faith was sandwiched between the divine commission to lead the Israelites into the land of promise and the continual wavering of that people's desire to enter the land.

What a heart for God Moses had! We see this reflected in the words, "Now therefore I pray thee, if I have found grace in thy sight, show me now thy way, that I may know thee, that I may find grace in thy sight: and consider that this nation is thy people" (Exod. 33:13). He desired to know God's way for His people and not his own way with that people. How easily is a leader's will imposed on God's people as seen in the highhanded appeals of ebullient monarchs of the electronic media, hawking their wares of human programs, personality, and propaganda.

Moses had that which was infinitely superior, "And the Lord spake unto Moses face to face, as a man speaketh unto his friend" (Exod. 33:11). Such a relationship is sorely needed in all of our lives, not simply for doing the work of the Lord, but more importantly for authenticating our lives and message by this vital touch with the living God. Yet Moses, the servant of God, was also blessed with a shepherd's heart.

In confrontation with those guilty of making and worshipping the golden calf, Moses stood, as a forerunner of Christ, between a judgment-deserving people and the Holy God. He told the people that he would meet with the Lord on their behalf, and in so doing he did not minimize the magnitude of their sin, "Oh, this people have sinned a great sin, and have made them gods of gold" (Exod. 32:31). At this point my wavering heart steps back from the resolve of Moses. I question that I could honestly say those words which came from the mouth of Moses as he stood as an intermediary for his people, "Yet now, if thou wilt forgive their sin—; and if not, blot me, I pray thee, out of thy book which thou hast written" (Exod. 32:32).

"Lord, I am their leader; their sins are mine. I must stand or fall with them." Here was no conniving, angle-working, ego-building leader. Here was true leadership, and all of us stand amazed at a spirit so foreign to our own! God spared Moses, though He dealt with those who had sinned.

That crucial issue resolved, Moses pleaded, "Go with us, Lord!" The reassuring words of the Lord came, "My presence shall go with thee, and I will give thee rest" (Exod. 33:14). Called meek, this Moses was really a bold man for, and before, God. He then answered the Lord in words which need to be emblazoned over every effort God's people ever undertake, "If thy presence go not with me, carry us not up hence" (Exod. 33:15).

What pastor would dare urge his flock to call a moratorium on their religious rat race in order to wait and be sure of the approval of God? He would be banished to the ecclesiastical hinterlands. With our mentality, we would have built pontoon bridges over the Jordan, organized tours of the Holy Land, or employed scuba equipment to cross the Jordan. But would we have said, "Stand still and see the salvation of our God!" That sounds like pietistic sloganeering to modern activists. If you question Moses' rationale, surely you would accept Christ's, "Without me ye can do nothing" (John 15:5).

Moses persisted in his dialogue with the Deity. He pointed out to the Founder of the nation that what distinguished Israel from all other peoples was "That thou goest with us." This very special incident pictures a man engaging in conversation with God Almighty. And the Lord answered Moses, "I will do this thing also that thou hast spoken: for thou hast found grace in my sight, and I know thee by name" (Exod. 33:17).

But this choice servant of God was not yet prepared to stop. Moses was pressing for a spiritual "bargain." He dared not lead this volatile people anywhere without the superintending presence of the Lord. Detecting that God was in "a blessing mood," he displayed his audacity with an awesome request, "I beseech thee, shew me thy glory" (Exod. 33:18). It is as if he wanted a rider appended to an already excellent bargain. How dare mere man negotiate with Deity!

This was a bold demand, but notice the fine print! He did not ask for himself some arbitrary power nor for some special gift (he could have used more skill as a public speaker). What he desired was to see the glory of God—God Himself. Neither what God could do for him, nor what he could do for God was Moses' concern. *He wanted God Himself!* Those four words may well state the longing and heart-cry of the practicing church. We seem to have everything else but His glory, that is, Himself. We try to bask in the ashen glow of men's glory, when we need desperately to be warmed by the glory of God.

To Moses' brazen request we would have said, "Sit down! You are going off the deep end, Moses"; yet one senses the holy pleasure of God to find a man interested more in His personality than in His power. "I will make all my goodness pass before thee" (Exod. 33:19). Of course Moses could not look upon the very essence of God. In his sin-beset nature he would have suffered some form of obliteration, "For there shall no man see me, and live" (Exod. 33:20). But Moses would see the "back parts of the glory of God," and that reflected glory would impact upon Israel for time immemorial.

There is a moving sequel to this. The man who had such intimate contact with God was unaware of its results. "Moses knew not that the skin of his face shone" with that reflected glory (Exod. 34:29). Aaron and the people saw, and Moses finally had to put a veil upon his face when he spoke to the children of Israel. It was not just the physical glow to which their eyes could not adjust, but the spiritual glow of a man who did "see" God and live, which was so overwhelming for them.

Nathaniel Hawthorne once wrote an intriguing story called, "The Minister with the Black Veil." A Puritan preacher appeared in his pulpit one Lord's Day, his face covered with a black veil never to be removed while he lived. Hawthorne did not tell why he wore it, but in the story the people conjectured as to whether he had been scarred or if he had sinned grievously and thus wore the veil in shame. They never found out. But the people of Israel knew why their prophet-priest-pastor wore his veil. It was because of his closeness to and their distance from God.

There is here no advocacy of duplicating someone else's experiences with God, but rather the concern that this living presence of God be something more than a tenet of orthodox theology. How ironic that Moses later lost his temper and thereby lost his opportunity to enter the land of promise. However, when the obituary notice for Moses was written following his unusual death while still at the zenith of his physical powers, what stood out in the minds of his people was something more significant than even the signs and wonders he performed in the land of Egypt. What greater tribute could have been penned than this: "And there arose not a prophet since in all Israel like unto Moses, whom the Lord knew face to face" (Deut. 34:10). There was so very much about Moses to be remembered, but this was the supreme measure of his life.

Reflect on the preceding. Does it have to be explained and applied? Have we not all occasionally been stopped in our tracks by an encounter with one of God's choice ones who radiated not a personality, but The Personality. We have all been around enough to know the difference. I recall the only time I ever heard A. W. Tozer speak. It was years ago in Buffalo, New York. I was surprised at first that he was not as tall as Goliath and then delighted by his homespun sense of humor. But most of all I was struck by the fact that here was a latter-day prophet whose message revealed an authority come from God. May we be blessed with such men in our generation!

Such can happen if we, too, first cry out, "Go with us, Lord!" Indeed, we are not short-changed in this vital matter of passing on the presence of God. We have an advantage over Moses, for since Pentecost God reveals Himself by indwelling our living temples when repentance and faith have been effected by the Holy Spirit. The writer of Hebrews alluded to this ultimate revelation in Christ as "being the brightness of his glory, and the express image of his [God's] person" (Heb. 1:3), and as the same One who indwells our lives.

A chain of life has been forged in the crucible of history, link by living link. John could say, "That which we have seen and heard declare we unto you, that ye also may have fellowship with us: and truly our fellowship is with the Father, and with his Son Jesus Christ" (1 John 1:3). Peter would add, "For we have not followed cunningly devised fables, when we made known unto you the power and coming of our Lord Jesus Christ, but were eyewitnesses of his majesty" (2 Pet. 1:16).

Our generation of believers must also pass on that unique presence of God—Christ in us—the hope of glory. For a Christian is one in whom Christ lives. This relationship is not static, but continuing. We are called upon to learn more about His personality, even as admonished by Peter, "But grow in grace, and in the knowledge of our Lord and Saviour Jesus Christ. To him be glory. . ." (2 Pet. 3:18). Is it not interesting that as Peter concluded a book concerned with apocalyptic matters, he concluded it so simply. No matter what goes on in the world, the blessed task of the believer is to cultivate this relationship to God through Christ and thereby reflect His glory in a darkening world.

But as the objective presence of God goes on in terms of His indwelling our lives, we must also desire an inner working which continually leads us to cry out, "Show us your glory, Lord!" Paul alluded to the situation in Moses' day in 2 Corinthians 3 and then proceeded to speak of how the glory of God became resident in the Corinthian believers, "For God, who commanded the light to shine out of darkness, hath shined in our hearts, to give the light of the knowledge of the glory of God in the face [person] of Jesus Christ" (2 Cor. 4:6). What a remarkable transformation had occurred in the lives of many of those Corinthians!

In our day, we do not veil the glory of God as Moses did; rather, our total beings are to flesh out the presence of God. There is now a special glory to be revealed, even as Paul described it, "But we all, with open face beholding as in a glass the glory of the Lord, are changed into the same image from glory to glory, even as by the Spirit of the Lord" (2 Cor. 3:18). Paul said that we are being "metamorphosed." We are changing from nonattractive caterpillars to lovely butterflies by the miracle of divine transformation. The scholars have debated what is here meant by glass or mirror. Most think it refers to the Word of God. Reflection on the written Word reveals the Living Word Who discloses the glory of God in our daily lives.

Many today would lead us to believe that such revealed glory should take on an aura of the exotic or ecstatic, almost a bizarre revelation of the power of God. Still, it is interesting to note that as the writer of Hebrews spoke of Christ as being God's "last word" or ultimate revelation, he spoke of the Lord as being the "exact expression of His Being." The word for expression or representation can be transliterated into English as the familiar word *character*.

Changing language reveals changing morals. Today to be a character is to be one who is different, in a negative sense. But not long ago, character related to basic and solid qualities of life which were commendable. It might not be a bad idea for some wings of the Church to ease off on their emphasizing the gifts of the Spirit while they allow the Lord to catch up in their lives with the fruit of the Spirit. The nine-fold description of the fruit of the Spirit in Galatians 5:22-23 is in essence old-fashioned character delineated in these terms: "Love, joy, peace, longsuffering, gentleness, goodness, faith, meekness, self-control."

Indeed, there needs to be a new manifestation of the presence of God. With Moses it was an outer radiance; with believers today it should be an inner radiance displayed in the fruit of the Spirit. That fruit gives validity to the gifts of the Spirit, even as our Lord's character gave credence to His miracles and teaching. This kind of presence ensures vitality and reality in the life of the individual and of the Church. There is no spiritual impudence intended to suggest that we rephrase Moses' plea, "Show me thy glory" with our plea, "Let us volitionally allow You, Holy Spirit, to show Your glory through us."

Eugene O'Neill, the famous author and playwright, died in 1979. On the occasion of his death, a memorial service was planned at which two well-known Broadway personalities were supposed to give readings from O'Neill's writings. The reporter covering the story did not hide his disappointment when these two individuals failed to make an appearance. The absence of their presence left an empty space and a hollow ring to the event.

Infinitely more significant, the absence of the presence of God leaves an empty place. The Christian does not have such emptiness in his life, for he knows the indwelling presence of the Lord. By preaching the gospel in Word and life, he passes on the presence of God to a needy world. But there is that manifestation of God we desperately need to enlighten our lives and kindle our hearts afresh for His service, and "That manifestation will be the difference between a nominal Christian life and a life radiant with the light of His face."

---

1. A. W. Tozer, *The Pursuit of God* (Harrisburg: Christian Publications, Inc., 1948), p. 64.

Epilogue

15

A Terrible Fury

"And they said to the mountains and to the rocks, 'Fall on us. . . .'" (Rev. 6:16, NASB).

Though not set in the apocalyptic context described by the Apostle John, May 18, 1980, will remain fixed in the minds of citizens of the Pacific Northwest as a day of staggering dimensions. May 18, 1980, was the day of the terrible fury of Mount St. Helens, when indeed a mountain fell on men.

A century of volcanic buildup exploded in a day as more than a cubic mile of material was discharged into the air—a ton of debris for every man, woman and child on the globe—and the top 1,270 feet of Mount St. Helens disappeared. What preceded that dizzying manifestation of natural force? Scientists calculated that inside the mountain an estimated 55 million tons of ground water—13 billion gallons—had collected at temperatures up to 424 degrees Fahrenheit, trapped between the surface and the approaching magma chamber like a giant pressure cooker.[1] And the lid was blown away as the climactic shock opened a crater two miles long and a mile wide, and unparalleled devastation levelled an area which had already been convulsed in the previous eight weeks by some 10,000 earthquakes. The terrible fury pulverized rock and sent a "stone wind" of 100 miles an hour across the immediate environs. Trees weighing tons went down as proverbial matchsticks before the force of that wind whose real speed, because of atmospheric conditions, was more like 300 miles an hour.

The grim reaper followed in the train of that cataclysmic onslaught as human beings and animals along with trees and countryside fell before its fury. Some of those who died of suffocation were later found to have succumbed from about a teacupful of ingested ash, a minute portion of the millions of tons of pulverized rock catapulted into the air on that unforgettable day.

Though the eruption soon became an international oddity and the focal point for much national attention, those who lived through or have seen the results of that day are still stunned by such destructive natural power. However, we cannot allow the event of Mount St. Helens simply to be filed away in geology textbooks, nor should we become concerned merely about possible future ash fallouts.

There is a theology of the mountain to be considered. The Christian needs to see lessons in this event. The universal response elicited from many in the region of the mountain was, "What is man?" How insignificant a creature he is thrust against the backdrop of such power. The psalmist carried the question to the ultimate, "When I consider thy heavens, the work of thy fingers, the moon and the stars, which thou hast ordained; What is man that thou art mindful of him?" (Ps. 8:3-4). Yet that spectacularly visible display of destruction must be balanced by the recollection of an equally overwhelming concept of construction. "By the word of the Lord the heavens were made, and by the breath of his mouth all their host," (Ps. 33:6). "What is man?" and what capacity does his mind have to grasp such a thought—immediate and measureless creation by the mere breathing of Deity?

The psalmist called on creation itself to praise the Lord, "For he commanded, and they were created," (Ps. 148:5). "Praise the Lord from the earth . . .stormy wind fulfilling his word: mountains and all hills. . ." (Ps. 148:7, 8b, 9a). Should not Mount St. Helens be a sign to this unbelieving generation? A fallen race, boasting of its weapons of overkill, has now been confronted by real energy, a terrible fury over which it has no control with no button to push or not push.

One would want to avoid linking the God who sent His Son to Calvary for our sins with the deaths of those slain by that "stormy wind"; still, Luther's puzzlement over what he called "the strange work of God" can lead us to an understanding of such an event as divine handwriting on the wall of nature to an arrogant, rebellious race.

Return to the consequences of that day. Giant boulders were found five miles from the mountain, coughed up from hundreds of feet inside Mount St. Helens, while rocks three stories high landed nearer to the site. The stone wind lashed out at D-8 caterpillar tractors three to ten miles away, stripping them of tracks and blades, shredding solid steel to confetti and scattering it for miles. Search teams and doctors performing autopsies on recovered victims described the results of that force on human bodies in terms we think best to omit from these pages.

The towering cloud of ash rose twelve miles over the volcano and left areas to the east awash in waves of ash. Cars self-destructed from the intake of that ash, people groped in a darkness akin to that of Pharaoh's day, and modern society screeched to a halt from the ashen sallies of Mount St. Helens. Millions of dollars of losses in crops, 120,000 acres of wasted forest land, serious damage to fish hatcheries, and the endless nuisance and cost of road cleanup have marked the volcano's target areas for years to come.

Countless are the stories of people who fled from the fury and of others who failed to heed warnings and entered too close to what would become the scene of their deaths. Foremost of these was Harry Truman, the blithe spirit of Spirit Lake, who urged reporters on May 11 to return and visit him. Spirit Lake was his home, and "I'll never leave it." But on May 18 a destructive force equalling 26.5 megatons of TNT swept out, burying him and his lodge beneath tons of debris and mud.

Controversy arose over the state of preparedness before the eruption, but who could have imagined what eventually happened? Somehow there was an attitude that "it won't happen," and no one could have conceived of the possibility that human beings would be disintegrated seven miles from the mountain or asphyxiated by volcanic ash sixteen miles away. Had the eruption occurred on May 17, many more would have died, for owners were allowed into the Red Zone that day to check on their property, though one wary state trooper said, "We hope the good Lord will keep that mountain from giving us any trouble."

Although far removed in terms of miles, Mount St. Helens and the Middle East remind us that we live in apocalyptic days. Even so, we all seem hypnotized by the routine of daily life. As one couple saw the eruption eleven miles away, they raced back in their vehicle to escape the ominous, black mass racing toward them. They warned one family whose members were casually preparing breakfast, but the warning went unheeded. The idea of warning in the Scriptures encompasses the thought of advance information, as well as of divine instruction. One of the classic illustrations relates to Noah: "By faith Noah, being warned of God of things not seen as yet, moved with fear, prepared an ark to the saving of his house; by the which he condemned the world, and became heir of the righteousness which is by faith" (Heb. 11:7). In so many words God had told Noah, "Something is going to happen to this earth!" Though ridiculed by his generation, Noah

141

responded to the warning and did something about it.

The prophets warned Israel and Judah with but moderate success. Joseph responded to divine warning and fled to Egypt with the child Jesus. John the Baptist warned his generation of the wrath to come, and Paul warned the Ephesian elders of doctrinally dangerous days ahead of them. To accept warning is to act in faith and see the unseen as real.

For years the Church has debated the minutiae of eschatology, but seldom has it taken seriously that mandate from the Mount of Olives, our Lord's clear warnings about the end times. Many have charted the chaos of the last days, but few have responded to the warnings of the Word of God and world events. We are like some of the photographers who wanted to get closer to Mount St. Helens for better pictures, but dismissed the warnings of wiser folk.

One "prophet" was present at Mount St. Helens, David Johnston the volcanologist. On March 28 he told a group of reporters, "This is an extremely dangerous place to be. If it were to erupt now, we would die." Less than two months later, he died at his post some five miles from the mountain. On that awesome day he shouted into his radio microphone, "Vancouver, Vancouver! This is it!. . ." He and his car simply vanished before that terrible fury.

As the Christian sees the clock of human history winding down, he must step briskly through life, knowing that time is running out and that it is not merely a prophetic cliché to sense, "that the coming of the Lord draweth nigh" (James 5:8). He awaits that trumpet call of God which will suddenly announce, "World, world, this is it. . .He is coming!"

How so Pauline that in the same context in which he wrote, "For when they shall say, Peace and safety; then sudden destruction cometh upon them. . .and they shall not escape," he could also say, "Now we exhort you, brethren, warn them that are unruly, comfort the feebleminded, support the weak, be patient toward all men" (1 Thess. 5:3, 14). The apostle grasped the future and its possibilities of danger, even as he was set to use the present in service to the Lord.

Let Mount St. Helens be a sign to man of the power of God and of the unpredictability of human life. Does our church generation long for signs? Then let this eruption also be a sign to the Church as to how puny man is in contrast with the power and the person of God. Indeed our age seeks to attain euphoria via an elixir distilled from the spirit of man, both the worldly and the churchly Adam. Yet, "What is man that Thou art mindful of him?"

Having heard, then let us heed the warnings of Scripture as we persevere in the work of the Lord (1 Cor. 15:58) and as we find peace in the words of the Lord: "God is our refuge and strength, a very present help in trouble. Therefore we will not fear, though the earth should change, and though the mountains slip into the heart of the sea; though its waters roar and foam, though the mountains quake at its swelling pride" (Ps. 46:1-3, NASB).

Let us also fall in worship and wonder at the feet of this One, our God and Savior—depicted by both a terrible fury and a marvelous grace—a Mount St. Helens and a Mount Calvary!

---

1. Acknowledgment is made of the use of some factual data in this chapter from the October 27, 1980, edition of the *Portland Oregonian*.